SUSS
THE
SYMMETRY

S U S S E D   C O.

First published in 2018 by Sussed Co., LLC
Text, Cover Design, and Illustrations © 2018 Samantha Smith

For permission requests email the publisher: hello@SussedCo.com

The content of this book is for general informational purposes only. It is not to be used for diagnosing or treating any medical condition or for replacing the services of your physician or other healthcare provider. The advice and strategies contained in the book may not be suitable for all readers. The terms 'we', 'us', 'you' and 'your' are made in their general form and not in specific reference to the reader or author. Please consult your healthcare provider for any questions that you may have about your own medical or emotional situation. Neither the author, publisher, nor any of their employees or representatives guarantees the accuracy of information in this book or its usefulness to a particular reader, nor are they responsible for any results, actions, or other consequences by any person reading this book.

ISBN-13: 978-0692129715

ISBN-10: 0692129715

Written and Illustrated by Sam Smith
Cover design by Sam Smith

Visit the Sussed Co. website www.SussedCo.com to learn more about Sussed Co. including books, events, coaching, and newsletter.

This book is dedicated to
all of the magnificent women
who occasionally implode.

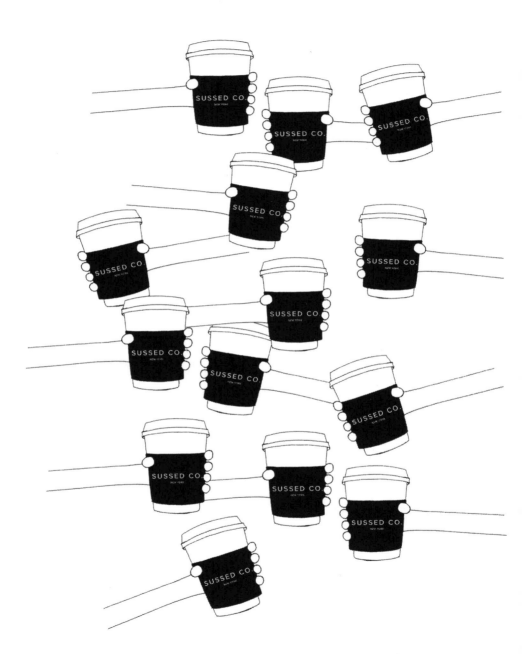

Suss | S · Us |

TRANSITIVE VERB

To figure out.

First use recorded in London, England, 1966

[British, informal]

We implode
and then
we grow.

If your imagination can take you to dark places and downtrodden perspectives, why on earth not nudge it along to somewhere better, and let it take you to somewhere inspiring and wonderful instead?

CONTENTS

CHAPTER ONE

SUSS YOUR SELF

CHAPTER TWO

SUSS THE SYMMETRY

CONTENTS

CHAPTER THREE
SELECT YOUR PERSPECTIVE

CONTENTS

CHAPTER FOUR
TAMING YOUR CONFIDENCE

CHAPTER FIVE
THE SUPPORT ORBIT

CONTENTS

CHAPTER SIX
THE SUSSED SIX

AND...

SAM SMITH

SUSS
THE
SYMMETRY

SAM SMITH

AUTHOR'S NOTE

I spent my twenties living in London devising creative and collaborative ideas and events for fashion and lifestyle companies amid a scene where nobody really had any idea that calming down once in a while might be a good thing.

One by one my friends and I hit our thirties and our infallibility began to fade. Modern day stresses, mental fatigue, multi-faceted living, fear of missing out at work and home, repeated over exertion in mind and body, obsessive tech rituals, and never taking our eyes off the future while persistently pushing the present can leave a woman so cool and so sorted in so many ways, with sketchy self-esteem, low confidence, shifty motivation, and old and cumbersome habits that appear and adhere like a sticker on her shoe whenever she's over-done or despondent and drained.

I occasionally wondered if we'd unleashed ourselves on life completely unprepared for the obstacles it was hurling.

I moved to New York in 2006 and bore witness once again to an increasing and accumulating pressure of social stress and the urge to 'have it all' (and more) that seemed to be sucking everyone around me into a vortex of bewilderment.

Women I knew and loved, from London to New York, were force-meditated from their highlights to their Saint Laurent star boots. They were also still over-extended, over-achieving, city-frazzled, socially hectic, side-affected from their own success... and adding more to the mix. Everyone was frantically searching for the elusive irony of 'balance'.

I got fed up of watching cool girls crumble and seeing fascinating women sporadically implode. I got fed up of my own incessant migraines. There was clearly a shift to be shaken.

I retrained as a Professional Life Coach, and Holistic Health Counselor and set myself the goal of creating an inspiring & progressive place to find, define, and refine 'balance' as a subjective pursuit.

Sussed Co. was born, Sussing the Symmetry evolved as a notion, and the backlash began.

These are the events that led to this book.

INTRODUCTION

This is a book about reclaiming self-awareness, unleashing the power of perspective, and boosting self-assurance in busy minds in a busy world.

It is about understanding who you are, what you want, and how you plan to carry yourself through it all.

It is about cracking the code on the ruts that can ruin a day, owning your hours, and spending them wisely.

When you Suss your Symmetry you choose the perspective you take rather than letting your perspective choose you. You begin to understand your trip wires, your triggers, and your propensity to turbulence.

You conjure a healthy disregard to the modern horror that is the feeling of being judged, the depleting plight of self-criticism and faltering confidence, and the urge to do everything like everybody else.

You establish and acknowledge the importance of an orbit of

support to keep you in an empowering place and nudge you further. And a force field of resourcefulness to suck up the threats that can throw your day.

IMAGINE THIS...

You engage the services of a (somewhat vulturous) assistant from a unique and mysterious agency. You've never done anything like this before, and you're not really sure what to expect, but everyone seems to be doing it lately, and you've already paid the deposit.

Your assistant arrives in a Tom Ford pencil skirt and black suede stiletto sling-backs and perches on your bed / desk / dinner table / bath tub, meticulously taking note of your likings and dis-likings, your paths and perspectives, your ins and outs, your riles and repercussions — all the things you neglect to notice because you're too busy being you.

She taps away at her laptop, fully determined to gather insight into your intricacies and power over your predilections to present an altogether more uplifting alternative to some of your daily dramas. This secures her some ongoing indispensability in your life, and her agency the juiciest client.

Sometimes, putting ourselves in somebody else's shoes, (particularly someone with permission to poke) can open our eyes and awaken the urge to shake off outdated behavior and rut-ish thought patterns in favor of something entirely more empowering.

So much of the time we know deep down what needs to be

done in our lives, but we lack the impetus for change. Or we sense the loom of an opposing pull and find it too seductive to stop the plunge.

For the purposes of your encounter with this book, you are that Vulturous Assistant. Entirely responsible for your own thoughts and decisions. You are also still you.

It is time to dig some claws into that life of yours.

INTRODUCING

ARABELLA GREENSTOCK

VULTUROUS ASSISTANT

Arabella Greenstock, fellow V.A (or Life Coach, if you like) is your mentor for the ride. Transcripts of her conversations are scattered throughout the pages of this book along with symmetry sussing tips, tricks, concepts, questions, and case-stories with the option to 'choose your own ending' — the purpose of which being to reinforce the alternative options in how things can end.

Many questions are asked, and ample space is provided at the back of the book for Vulturous Assistant notes and ideas.

Change should be enchanting, and it is my endeavor as a writer to use fiction (by way of the various dramas of a cast of fictitious characters) to emphasize the power of perspective in a situation. Sometimes our own awareness is heightened by observing the predicaments of others.

It should be noted that the conversational technique of Ms. Greenstock is only loosely inspired by the mechanics of Professional Life Coaching. Arabella's style is altogether more inquisitive and propositional than a professional rule-adhering Life Coaching conversation would be.

A Professional Coach will 'coach the client and not the story'. That is, she will ask carefully curated questions based upon achieving the objective set forth by her client at the start of the session, whatever it may be - snag a prince, win a million, mix a martini, drop 10lbs eating cake...

The coach will not direct her client or pass judgment or assumption on what she feels the clients goal or path ought to be. Arabella Greenstock, by contrast, delves into the detail, steers the subject and dishes out the occasional accompanying social commentary.

That said, the emphasis of a thought-provoking and creative partnership rings true to traditional coaching practice and definition, and it is this creative collaboration which conjures so much of the magic of potential in both fiction and reality.

It is because of these modifications and the self-application of the pursuit that the role has evolved as a Vulturous Assistant as opposed to a Life Coach.

Formalities out of the way, congratulations. Welcome aboard. You can start right away. Footwear and laptop optional.

THE VULTUROUS ASSISTANT

EMPLOYEE HANDBOOK

DEPARTMENT PROTOCOL

RULE ONE

BE
HONEST
WITH
YOURSELF

We sometimes repackage our 'truth' for purpose, motive, or palatability. This book is pulsating with questions to pose to yourself. Sometimes you might need to keep asking the same question again and again to get to your real truth.

The 'truth' is something that varies for all of us. We all have our own version of 'truth', unlike the often confused and far more rigid counterpart, the 'fact'.

Sometimes the truth can hurt, especially if we feel we have done something wrong, or something embarrassing, or it means admitting to fear or regret.

But, owning is empowering, and that is the place where we start to suss ourselves, acknowledge the previous imbalance, lift the mist, and select the next perspective.

RULE TWO

RETREAT
TO
CONQUER

.

Stepping away from expectation and comparison, keeping up, and fear of missing out, obsessive tech rituals, overloading schedules and overbearing people provides the pause and peace to think.

Modern schedules can often leave no time to think. Thinking seems to have been squeezed out between more fashionable rituals of meditation and mindfulness, or attention deficient cell-phone overuse.

Answer yourself on an empty mind, away from influence.
Time to comfortably think is essential in Sussing Yourself.

RULE THREE

ACCEPT
AND
RESPECT
FLEXIBILITY

We sometimes approach the notion of change with a mindset that whatever changes we make in our lives will be forever. This can be daunting and stifling and enough of a fright to stop us before we start.

Positive change should be enchanting and empowering and entrenched in the knowledge that it is in our control. This means we can always change our minds.
For changes to work they need to feel right and feeling forced rarely does that.

Accepting flexibility allows for creative modification. One size never fits everyone; hence the advocacy of 'symmetry' as a subjective pursuit.

RULE FOUR

ACKNOWLEDGE
THE
SMALL
STUFF

When a day can turn on the power of a seemingly small and superficial object or event, when there are big things happening 'out there' in the world, we can be reluctant to identify and address it because it seems silly and inferior.

The stories and conversations used throughout this book were written to show the power that perspective can have on the various chunks that comprise an average day, and how, when the chunks are 'chunked' together, those perspectives can gain in impact and influence, rolling over onto each other and knocking into patience, confidence, relationships, energy, ability, assurance, and motivation.

It builds.

When our responses are entrenched in ruts of old we can conjure ingrained, on-repeat, auto-pilot perspectives towards situations and occurrences. They are the knee-jerk reactions. They don't have to be that way.
When we become aware of the power of the perspectives we

take, and the riles that lead to repercussions in our lives, we are liberated to choose to experience alternative perspectives instead.

LOVE SPREADS

The obstacles and predicaments faced in the stories on these pages will be considered by some as supremely peripheral and insignificant in relation to the plight faced by some of the people on this planet, and indeed the plight faced by many of us in our daily lives. Yet, I argue that we should not disparage by comparison when we have the opportunity to use these examples to increase our own sense of awareness, and to open the gates of potential to wrestle ourselves better perspectives.

When we suss the small stuff the potential for greater change is unleashed, not just for us, but for those around us, and even for those around them.

FOR EXAMPLE...

We can spend our days irritated by inept baristas, or we can raise our self-awareness and acknowledge that, yes, it might be a bit embarrassing, but a crappy coffee in the morning might just be something that prods us and has the potential to poke into our further experience of the day, and therefore it well warrants the working out of a solution and a subsequently more empowering perspective.

For the big picture, out there on the planet; if we have a joint goal of making this crumbling world a better, stronger, more peaceful and purposeful place, then we are surely far better placed to do so if we're not, for example, shriveling under guilt over something we said last week, or annoyed because we've just hauled ourselves out of the bath tub to answer the phone to a marketing robot, or irritable because our underwear elastic has been weaving its way between our butt cheeks all afternoon.

CAST WISELY

Get peeved, but do so with purpose, and know your way out. Doing so leaves us in a better position to support positive change all around us. And that means we are stronger to do something about the big stuff.

Most of us combine a few chemical reactions in our cauldrons and conjure up spells to last us the day.

Know the power of your potions and the strength of your spells. Cast wisely.

·

THE INTRODUCTION OF

ARABELLA GREENSTOCK VULTUROUS ASSISTANT

NEW YORK CITY

·

Arabella Greenstock sat down at her desk. Her office was the whitewashed space she had imagined for herself when she'd embarked on this journey. She still had the letter in her desk drawer. The one she had written to her future self. The one in which she'd described, quite embellished in its detail, what she believed was important in life, who she wanted to become, what she needed to conquer, and how it looked when she had.

Gradually day by day, week by week, year by year, the letter had evolved into the blueprint that she had, give or take a page or two, made happen. It had become a passionate piece of self-awareness; a sort of paper equivalent of one of those rousing compilations of video clips that television people assemble and add to emotional music to commemorate major events, and which turns those events into something that everyone looks back on with great sentimentality and surging emotion.

'What bigger event,' Arabella was fond of saying, 'is there than your own life?' She earnestly encouraged her clients to pepper their lives with rousing music.

Occasionally, Arabella wondered if any of it would have been possible without the repertoire of setbacks that she had in her past. Those things she used to assume held her down with invisible pins, but had, with a change of perspective, turned out to propel and inspire her. She thought not.

'If your imagination can take you to dark places and downtrodden perspectives,' she would tell her clients, 'then it is equally capable of the reverse. Why on earth not nudge it along to somewhere better and let it take you to somewhere inspiring and wonderful instead?'

Arabella opened her planner and looked at the day ahead. She pulled open a thick folder of client files and flicked through them. They were all extremely beautiful women, although many of them didn't think so.

They were all extremely clever women, although some of them in ways that can be disregarded depending on who is wielding the power to judge.

They were all highly capable, although some of them were riddled with insecurity. Or pushing themselves so far and fast that they barely knew where they were.

They were all completely unique, although many of them fought for the safety of feeling the same.

They were often so busy tuning into each other that they forgot to tune into themselves.

They were all extremely complex, and most of them knew exactly where their fault lines lay, but for whatever reason they repeatedly tripped over them.

Arabella sipped her coffee, winced, for it was a bad cup of coffee, and buzzed in her first appointment of the day.

CHAPTER ONE

SUSSING YOUR SELF

The start of it all is to Suss Your Self. Sussing who you are does not mean dissecting every atom and occurrence in your existence. It means gaining a functional working knowledge of you as a unique and individual person in order to make your reality more productive and satisfying.

The reality in life is that bits of it are, of course, pretty tricky and thus they may, at times, remain.
But, you can master your experience of it; from self-depreciating or bleak perspectives to unfavorable comparisons. From crappy clothes days, to soaking up the mood swings or expectations of others. From fear filled ruts, to frenetic antics.

It's all out there for our powers of perception to filter and condense into experience, and it is that experience that we have the power to morph into something entirely more enchanting and energizing.

There can sometimes be a tendency to overlook the most very basic questions in life in favor of simply 'getting on with it'. Situations can sweep us away. Time is short and the current is strong. Before you know it, its ten years later and you wonder how you got there.

If you stop and acknowledge the present - if you Suss Your Self - you empower yourself to override some of the struggles that don't fit into the 'bigger picture'. You lessen the strength of the tide. You choose which way you swim, and even the color and cut of your swimwear.

But how to start?

.

SUSSED SELF SOFTWARE

.

Sussing yourself is like running a piece of self-software for the post-digital age. Something that runs in the background all day and all night, un-intrusive, unobtrusive, apart from the potential to refocus an outlook to a perspective that is better, brighter, clearer and more 'together'. Something more in tune with the life you want and the way you'll get it.

It is the sort of software to be activated at some point before embarking on the day ahead, 'before the bra,' so to say.

The sort of software that can anticipate a problem before it happens (because it has probably happened before).

The sort of software that spits out a daily report...

This is who I am...

This is what I need...

This is what is important to me...

This is what today needs to be about...

This is what I will do if it doesn't go to plan...

This how I plan to carry myself through it all...

Sussed Self Software is the act of pre-setting intention for the day ahead. It is a purpose filled pause before autopilot can interrupt.

The objective is to increase self-awareness, purpose, and perspective of what really matters, how we want our lives to be, and how we need to feel and act to get there. This is Perspective Power for the Bigger Picture.

·

SUSS YOUR SELF

THE VULTUROUS ASSISTANT REPORT

·

Then there is the Vulturous Assistant Report. A more detailed affair, where she'll follow you for days (you wish she wouldn't come into the bathroom).

She'll witness your irritations, your surges of happiness, what happens when you have too much of one thing, or too little of another.

Through time and inquisition...

She knows what it takes to throw your day

And what you need to get it back on track again

SHE'S SEEN HOW MUCH YOU SLEEP, AND HOW MUCH YOU WEIGH

She's seen what you eat

And how you eat it

She's seen how you interact, what you believe in

SHE'S SEEN WHO AND WHAT HAS THE POWER TO IRK YOU, OR TO BOIL YOUR BLOOD

She knows what you stand for, and what you feel is important.

She knows what worries you, who you love, who you adore and who you could do without

She knows how you treat your family, colleagues, friends, and strangers

She sees the time you invest in the

various fragments that comprise
your day

SHE KNOWS WHAT REALLY ANNOYS YOU ABOUT
OTHER PEOPLE

And what you find completely enchanting.

SHE SEES THE FADS YOU GET SUCKED INTO...

...and the depth of your fear of missing out

SHE KNOWS WHAT YOU LOVE ABOUT YOUR DAY

And what you could do without

She knows what your dreams are, even if you have forgotten them yourself

SHE KNOWS YOUR FEARS

She knows what you believe about yourself that just isn't true

SHE KNOWS WHAT YOU CARE ABOUT

And what you wish didn't bother you

And also, what you wish mattered to
you a bit more

She knows what motivates you.

And what leaves you cold

She knows what would make you shudder to think you might still be doing in five years' time

She knows what you'd do if you felt there were no barriers

She knows exactly who you'd love to tell to get stuffed

SHE KNOWS THE THINGS YOU FEEL GUILTY ABOUT

And if you are justified or not

SHE KNOWS THE PEOPLE, PLACES, AND POTIONS THAT INFLUENCE YOUR IDEAS ABOUT THE WORLD

She knows your riles

AND YOUR REPERCUSSIONS

She knows about all of your subliminal snags

She knows how you like to punish yourself

...AND WHEN THE SENTENCE EXCEEDS THE MISDEMEANOR

She knows what suits you about your lifestyle

SHE KNOWS WHERE YOU SQUANDER YOUR TIME

She knows the dreams you gave up on

And if you should wake them up

She knows if you know the value of the hours in your day

...AND IF YOU SPEND THEM WISELY ENOUGH.

She knows if you get sucked into other people's mood swings

She knows the mist you need to lift to get where you want

She knows which of your perspectives in life are your own

AND WHICH BELONG TO SOMEONE ELSE

She perches on the side of your desk / bed / sofa / bathtub and opens her report...

What does she say?

...AND WHAT DO YOU TELL HER SHE'S MISSED?

CASE STORIES

ONE
WOMAN'S
MANTRA

CHOOSE YOUR OWN ENDING

Gia sat down and looked around her. She had a nervous smile which, if she used it for long enough, would result in a headache that would last all day. Gia was never aware she was doing that smile until she felt the tingle of the headache start to erupt. The smile had a mind of its own, appearing when she was anxious or surrounded by people who bored her (but by whom she kindly wanted to appear interested). It was the sort of smile a child will do when someone points a camera in their face and demands of them 'cheese'.

Alas, nobody today was smiling in response. All around her women were sitting down, folding their coats in their laps, or arranging and re-arranging them on the backs of their chairs, re-sipping re-usable water bottles and plucking phones out of their bags under the guise of pre-occupation; the perfect reason not to shatter the invisible glass between strangers.

Gia wholeheartedly regretted signing up for today. 'Find Yourself' it was called. How apt that she now found herself lost amid an auditorium of a thousand other, presumably also lost women.

Would she find herself? Perhaps, which seemed more likely,

she should search various lost property departments from the successive portions of her life, which had led, collectively, to the feeling of being somewhat dissolved alive. It would be laborious, true, but certainly cheaper than this course. But, there was no refund for cancellations, that had been made very clear. So here she was.

The lights dimmed. The music began. A smoke machine chugged out a cloud of mystery and the front three rows covered their noses with their sleeves. A woman leapt onto the stage. When the fog partially cleared Gia could see that she wore a striped leotard and leggings like a 1980's fitness instructor.

The only sign of the times was the headset, which emitted a screech. The crowd cheered. Some went wild. Some stood to applaud. Everyone looked full of hope and anticipation that whatever cracked confidence had brought them there was going to be wiped away by the swipe of a star jump from a stranger on the stage.

'I'm Lulu! Your warm up!' the woman said with great high-pitched enthusiasm. 'Dawn is minutes away!' This spurred more cheering. Dawn O'Hope was the self-appointed guru and social media sensation and founder of the 'Find Yourself' movement.

Lulu encouraged the crowd to 'get some physical' with their neighbor. Gia ducked her head in her bucket back and pretended to ferret for something important. She sensed her two neighbors uncomfortably embracing over the top of her collapsed body. This was Gia. Always the outsider. Never quite comfortable 'team building' or dancing at parties, or 'getting some physical' with strangers. How on earth was she ever going to 'find herself' hidden in a bucket bag?

'Man!' I'm feeling that love!' Cried Lulu. 'Love is everything!'

'Woooooop!' shrieked several women in response. 'Love is You!' Cried Lulu and more cheers erupted.

'We are going to do some affirmation aerobics!' She continued. 'Get you all feeling really good! Reallllllyyy Gooooood! Get you in the mood! In tune with the world. In tune with the music. Warrrmmmmmmm!'

'Now say after me; "I am beautiful!'
'I am beautiful.' replied around a quarter of the audience half-heartedly.
'I am beautiful!' Cried Lulu.
"I am beautiful!' replied another ten percent.

It carried on this way. The whole room, apart from Gia, was eventually saying they were beautiful. True, it was in varying degrees, clearly some of the women believed it, but others were crying, which raised Gia's doubts. The smoke machine malfunctioned over all that beauty and bellowed a cloud of pollution. 'Cut that f***ing machine off! Cut it off! Get it out of here! Get it out!' Lulu hissed with venom, clearly audible over her head set. 'Cut it off!' shouted a few misguided audience members, thinking this was the next affirmation. 'Get it out!'

Several attempts were made to remove the rusting convulsing spluttering contraption from the stage before the sprinkler system let loose over the auditorium.   Still, there were people 'feeling the love' 'dancing in the rain' embracing strangers. 'Getting some physical'.
Finding themselves.

It's all about perception.

And the ability to resonate.

'Find Yourself' was halted abruptly. Lulu tried to tell everybody how to find her on social media as the auditorium spilled out onto the cold streets of a Manhattan winter. Several people were now being treated for smoke inhalation, three had panic attacks, a good third of them were still shouting affirmations, two were detained by the police for demanding passing strangers 'Get it out.'

Gia Meanwhile....

CHOOSE
YOUR
OWN
ENDING

PERSPECTIVE ONE

Gia was utterly euphoric with relief that it was over early and went straight to a hotel bar that she usually only went to on the special occasions of other people. It was dark, warm, and it smelled of candles and nighttime. It felt decadent and delicious for a Saturday afternoon. There was a seat in front of an open fire. The rest of the place was packed. She sat and the server asked what she wanted. She almost said, 'to find myself' but instead she asked for a Watermelon Martini. She wasn't due home for another three hours and it was here, in this bar, alone, digging into the depths of her bucket bag and pulling out a battered novel she'd been wanting to read for months, that she suddenly felt more like herself again. Slightly sussed, semi-'found.'

OR

PERSPECTIVE TWO

Gia trudged home despondently. This was her last hope to find herself and she couldn't even get with the affirmation. When she arrived back at her apartment her husband, who hadn't been expecting her for another two hours, was asleep on the couch. The three-year-old was drawing great swirling circles on the wall in red crayon and the toddler was drinking the dregs of an upended cappuccino. Sports was blaring out of the TV. Waffles clung syrup side down onto the shag pile rug.

Gia pondered back-stepping it back out of the apartment again, but then the three-year-old stopped his graffiti and spun around to face his mother. "See what happens when you're gone?" he deadpanned at Gia, who suddenly realized, that for all of the changes, she wasn't lost at all. Just transported. Far too quickly. Into another phase of life.

And there would be more to come.

.

SUSS YOUR SELF

ONE WOMAN'S MANTRA

.

We 'get' things in different ways, and in different capacities. Mantra's work a treat for millions of women and millions of others will only ever feel like they are trying to trick themselves.

One woman's mantra is another's misery.
One woman's affirmation is another's irritation.
So be it.
Accept, acknowledge, and so be aware, that the sussing of oneself is an entirely subjective pursuit, one that is always open to change as we evolve and life goes on. There are plenty of good perspectives to take on the bad.
You get to choose your own ending every time.

.

SUSS YOUR SELF

SUSS
THE
AIR

.

In cracking the code on the ruts that can ruin a day, in owning hours (and spending them wisely), and in understanding who we are and what we want out of life, we need to consider - with great importance - how we want to carry ourselves through it all.

Sometimes we carry ourselves without thought, simply because we are too busy getting things done.
Other times we might carry ourselves in the ways to which we have become subconsciously accustomed over time - the subway glare, the nervous slump...

But, we have a choice.
Part of Sussing Your Self is to Suss the Air with which you carry yourself.

For example; many women do not walk around with grins plastered on their faces. It would be impractical, uncomfortable, and (some might say) provocative to do so. Many women simply walk around wondering what they've got to do next, and then what they've got to do after that. These thoughts are occasionally interrupted, in public places, by annoying leering condescending male voices saying 'smile!' and sometimes 'it might never happen!' (I've never heard a woman say either of these things to a stranger on the street). The energy that it takes for an already exhausted woman to quash the urge to flatten the purveyor of such a statement is immense. It would use vital reserves. This, and (joke) the risk of arrest, is largely why she doesn't. It certainly does not propel her to 'smile'.

Our perspectives in life cannot be demanded of us any more than our smiles can be demanded of us while we walk down the street.

Our perspectives have to be conjured from within, and once we realize we have a choice, all manner of opportunity starts to begin.

But, entrenched in old habits, how can we see there's a choice? 'Sussing the Air' is a process by which we decide, in advance or in the moment, how we want to carry ourselves through an event or occurrence.

It is a thoroughly Modern Deportment; less posture, more perspective. Sometimes inspired by the way we know we want to feel instead, and sometimes inspired by way of inspiration from a momentary mentor: someone admired in life, history, the media...

What do we admire about them exactly? Perhaps they are...

Brave?

COURAGEOUS?

Ground Breaking?

Determined?

EVOLVING?

No Nonsense?

Honest?

KIND?

Riddled with panache?

Pioneering?

Persistent?

Unafraid?

COOL AS A CUCUMBER?

Serene?

LIKE SUNSHINE?

OPTIMISTIC?

PATIENT?

BOLD?

nonchalant?

outgoing

UNFLAPPABLE?

CREATIVE?

QUICK-WITTED?

Stubborn

ENCHANTING?

motivated

POISED?

DON'T SNACK BETWEEN MEALS?

what exactly?

We then consider if the qualities and character traits we have identified aren't far from ones we might like to embody for ourselves that day, or for whatever particular endeavor we face. If they are, then we set ourselves some intention to try them for size and see how it feels.

It's all about perspective.

CHAPTER TWO

SUSSING THE SUMMETRY

Balance is a buzzword. The search for 'balance' can be the root of much impatience, anxiety, over and under indulgence, stress, panic, and discontent in the modern western world as we strive to procure it, stash it, and sit on top of it feeling smug and glossy limbed, in a difficult yoga pose, with perfect hair.

Searching for 'balance' is made mystical and beguiling because the urge to 'seek' it inevitably only comes when we've been left somewhat crumbled and lacking. Thus, it could be argued, rendering the search for balance a stress in itself.

It is made harder still by the fact that most of us know exactly what everybody else is up to (or want us to think they are up to) thanks to the personal propaganda machine that is rampant social media.   That can lead us to think that if we were doing it too, (whatever 'it' might be), then everything would be ok and life would fall into place...

'Balance' is highly ambiguous, and other people's balance is catnip to the time short and city frazzled. People move in packs. Just like when somebody starts running and then everyone is at it, or drinking a certain drink, or wearing ath-leisure with their high heels out to dinner, or freezing off their fat, or watching, wearing, reading or listening to something that everyone else is doing. Studies show that respondents to a quiz will put the wrong answer if the person next to them writes it first. Humans want to fit in. Even when it means writing the wrong answer.

But real balance is a subjective pursuit.

Sussing the Symmetry is a retreat from the idea that you ought to be doing or thinking things just because other people are. It is a state of self-awareness and perspective that allows us to find, define, and refine what is right for us. And an open mind that things can always change.

·

SUSSING THE SYMMETRY CASE STORIES

SUSS
THE
SYMMETRY

THE WORKSHOP

·

Arabella Greenstock's 'Suss the Symmetry' workshops were almost always over-subscribed. It was as if her participants expected to arrive and enter some sort of space age processing device, then be spat back out onto the steamy Manhattan sidewalk two hours, 500ml of bottled water and two coffees later, freshly refined and defined and sussed.

The irony of her workshops, Arabella often thought, was that if she got to speak a bit more, then they might. But then, she thought conversely, perhaps the magic occurred when they, as a group, combined to spurt their asymmetric ideas, and ignited, inspired or irritated each other into leaving resolved to do what resonated to them and them only.

The topics that stimulated such transformation were usually highly unanticipated, but always began the same way:

"LET'S TALK ABOUT BALANCE"

The Group: Many of whom had been texting, tweeting, scrolling, and buying things with their cell phones are suddenly alert.

Maureen: I cannot tell you the time, energy and money I have spent searching for balance.

Maeve: Me too. It exhausts me.

Celine: Like a lost dog... Lost balance. $2000 reward.

Mavis: I'd pay more than $2000.

Sarah: Did you know it's harder to balance with your eyes closed?

Claire: You know those days... Your alarm goes at 4am, you're so tired that you blend the scoop of the protein powder into the smoothie. Then you start a reluctant and stressful meditation session that keeps getting interrupted by your to-do list in your head, and finally gets interrupted by your kids, who got woken up by the blender blade hacking up the plastic scoop, and they want to play, and you yell at them, which is really un-Zen, and they both start to cry and you feel awful, but have to leave them crying in the doorway because you've registered for a fitness class at 5am and then you shower after the class and go straight to the office and realize you left your laptop in the locker room and you barely get any work done because you are trying to get hold of your laptop, and you keep sending nice text messages to the nanny to show the kids because you still feel guilty about shouting at them, but you just know that that the nanny won't show them to the kids, so you send a bitchy text about the nanny to your friend and you're still trying to get hold of your laptop and before you know it you've sent a message about the nanny to the nanny and then you spend the whole afternoon wondering if the nanny will walk out and you'll have to find another nanny. Which takes forever, so you end up eating a dry cupcake leftover from an office birthday and might as well have not even bothered with the gym.... you know those days?

Malia (circled by three small children intermittently being handed snacks and told to 'go and play with your brother'): No.

Lavinia: I've got a blender. I've been blending for a week and I thought I'd feel better than this. I'm miserable. I'm bloated. I fart constantly. I have never spent so much money on vegetables in my life, or enjoyed them less. And I'm anti-social because all I talk about is pesticides...

Caroline: But you post all of those lovely photos of smoothies on your Squareheart profile...

Lavinia: I spend most of the day getting the photo right. I'm so behind on everything after I finally do that I panic, then I keep checking to see if anyone's liked the picture, then I worry if they haven't. Then I have to clean the blender which takes so long I usually give up half way through and and leave it in the sink where it stares at me all day, fossilizing with flax seeds and kale leaves and reminding me of failure.

Sarah: Hashtag 'balance'.

Claudia (in very thinly veiled humor): I'd love to have enough time to stare at a blender all day...

Arabella: The notion of balance seems to scare the lot of you. You perpetually seek it, invest in it, get panicked by it. What if you found a new term for a new perspective? A new term, on your terms, what if your goal was Sussing the Symmetry instead of seeking balance? What could happen then? Might it seem less daunting and pressurized? Less of a uphill struggle?

Claudia (sarcastically): Arabella Greenstock and the rebranding of balance...

Michelle: Juices are the only reason I don't get sick in the winter.

Chloe: I love that 5am class. It sets me up for the day ahead.

Paulette: It's so hard to get into.

Claire: That's the only reason I go to it.

Paulette: Because it's so hard to get into?

Claire: Yes, and my friends can't.

Anna (to Claire): Do you ever think you'd have had a better day if you'd stayed in bed?

Riley: But how would she exercise? She works all day. She has two kids...?

Suzette: What's wrong with the European way of just walking a lot and holding in your stomach?

Ella: Is that what they do? I'd feel like everyone around me was toning up and I was toning down if I didn't work out so hard that I was in constant threat of an injury.

Claudia: Fitness Roulette?

Arabella: So, do you all work out the way you do for yourselves or for other people?

Ella: I don't really know. I'm too tired to think.

Dara (desperate to contribute and on the edge of her seat): I blend kale with spinach, chard, collard greens, dandelion leaves, adaptogenic herbs, almonds and filtered water. I'd never touch a protein powder, they are processed junk. You might as well blend your shoe into your smoothie if you're using protein powders. I can feel the energy from the sun and the vitamins from the soil in every leaf I devour. I conduct my day fueled by nature.

Arabella: This is what I'm talking about – Symbolism – Dara has created symbolism around her morning smoothie. She believes in its glow. She 'feels' it and it will undoubtedly fuel her. It might seem bizarre to everyone else but she doesn't care. She's doing Life Her Way.

Lola: Mind over matter?

Ella: (frantically taking notes) When did we move onto Symbolism?

Gita: The leaf thing scares me a bit.

Anouk: And gas forming.

Ella: They give me diarrhea.

Suzette: The greens? They make me fart.

Debbie: I always have to pretend it's my dog... or one of the children.

Dara: You shouldn't hide your farts. Farting is feminist.

Arabella: Feminism is often lost in translation, don't you think Dara? Although, If farting in public empowers you...

Dara: Actually, yes.

(All shift chairs slightly away from Dara).

Anouk: The green juices are really healthy. They make up for the computer screens.'

Dara (Sipping a dark green liquid with a pulse): Well, I don't care what any of you think, I love it.

Arabella: Brilliant, Dara! Love it. Live your own life Ladies. It won't be forever.

SUSS THE SYMMETRY
OWN YOUR HOURS

The time short and City Frazzled notoriously scrimp and pinch their hours so lean that days are productively sliced and proportioned; each piece over-serving a purpose and anything 'wasted' frustratingly conceded as a failure.

This is the realm of 'having it all' which, by the very nature of the word 'all' can't fail to consider also being permanently on the edge of the sense you might be about to implode.

Will a green juice fix that? Maybe a coffee? Or another exercise session, a meditation? Just for balance... but after you've ordered some laundry detergent, and picked up the dry cleaning and started on dinner.

How did you get there? When did the boundaries blur on how much you could handle?

Time is the same wherever you go. It can be an intriguing thought to consider since we all spend time so differently.

The stature of time effectively spent is an entirely subjective pursuit, or it would be if we achieved complete truth with ourselves and genuine self-awareness in our self-interest and intent for how we choose to spend it.

Owning Your Hours is accepting the fact that there are twenty-four of these things in a day, and if you are blessed to experience each of them in health and safety, then you have a responsibility to appreciate, and not depreciate, their value.

If you were to engage the services of your Vulturous Assistant, how would she consider you currently Own Your Hours?

How would she rate you on Parallel Hours? - Those hours spent worrying, growling, scrolling, dwelling, bitching, fretting, fearing, skirting, avoiding - the time we neglect to acknowledge that counts. It still ticks away.

How would she rank your Over or Under-Done Hours? - Those hours that are spent on accepted necessities, but sometimes in unnecessary long or short amounts.

What about your Uneasy Hours? - The time spent dreading vs doing. Did you ever stop to think that it all adds up as time spent?

How many of your hours are spent living Life Your Way? - in a manner that reflects your Self Software:

This is who I am...
This is what I need...
This is what is important to me...
This is what today needs to be about...
This is what I will do if it doesn't go to plan...
This how I plan to carry myself through it all...

In Vulturous Assistant style, from the side, with permission to poke, how do you Own your Hours?

How do you spend your food hours?

Are you distractedly overlapping them with other activity?

Or hastily erasing them at your desk so that you've already finished your lunch before you've noticed you've begun?

WHAT ABOUT EXERCISE? DOES YOUR MOVEMENT OF CHOICE BRING YOU VITALITY, HEALTH, AND HAPPINESS

OR IS IT GRUDGINGLY SPENT, WILLED OVER AND DREADED?

How do you sleep? Would your Vulturous Assistant suggest that your lifestyle has anything to do with your answer?

DO YOU EVEN NOTICE THE SMALL AND SURPRISING MOMENTS THAT LIFT YOUR PERSPECTIVE AND INCREASE YOUR SELF-ASSURANCE?

Do you spend enough time acknowledging yourself for what you do well?

What about the power of hours in advance?

HOW MUCH TIME DO YOU SPEND STEWING ON THINGS THAT HAVEN'T HAPPENED YET?

Or on dwelling on things that have already have?

DOES IT SEEM A FAIR OR EXCESSIVE AMOUNT?
DOES IT SERVE A PURPOSE?

DOES YOUR VULTUROUS ASSISTANT FEEL YOUR
APPROACH IS PRODUCTIVE?

Does it help or hold you back?

WHAT DO YOU LOOK FORWARD TO DOING?

What do you endure reluctantly?

What does she think about that?

COULD THAT TIME BE RECLAIMED AND REINVESTED
FOR MORE PURPOSE?

WHAT ABOUT YOUR RUTS? THOSE PLACES YOU GET STUCK IN, THE MINDSETS
ON REPEAT, THE AUTO-PILOT ATTITUDES AND ACTIONS THAT HOLD YOU BACK -
HOW MUCH TIME DO THEY SUCK FROM YOUR DAY?

HOW MUCH TIME DO YOU SPEND REWARDING
YOURSELF FOR RUT-ADDLED BEHAVIOR?

If you were to write a letter to yourself from the future that you
want for yourself, would your current Hour Ownership reflect the
way to get there?

SUSS THE SYMMETRY
HOURS

Hours. We are given 24 every day. Sometimes that can seem like far too much, but more often it feels like far too little. In Sussing the Symmetry we need to appreciate the value of the hours in our days as if they were currency. They express the value of our lives.

Spend them wisely.

·

CASE STORIES

A MODERN GLUTTONY IN AN AGE OF WELLNESS

CHOOSE YOUR OWN ENDING

·

It had been a long day. In the busy subway ride home after work Diana, shunted into someone's armpit, had held her breath for an entire stop. Extracting herself panting with relief as the carriage finally pulled to a stop and emptied out, her first thought was that she was finally free to pluck her phone from her bag, and with no particular reason other than habit, she entered her passcode and wondered what to do next.

Somewhat later on, back at her apartment, after four consecutive episodes of a television drama that she wasn't sure she liked but felt compelled to watch because other people thought it was wonderful, Diana pulled herself wearily off the sofa and made a half-hearted attempt at the seven step Korean cleansing regime that was running a craze on the internet. She got to the third step before the pull of perfect skin lost its grip. She picked up her phone and absentmindedly continued preparing for bed.

Waking abruptly, seemingly moments after she had eventually fallen asleep, Diana sleepily dragged herself out of bed and wandered into the bathroom, where she sat down on the toilet seat and started to pee the 500ml of filtered water she had hastily drunk four hours before, when, while brushing her teeth, her phone had dismally alerted her to the fact that she was way behind in her daily hydration target.

She pulled out the charging cable from the socket and watched the screen light up, noting with satisfaction that several new strangers were now 'following' her on Squareheart, and also, with less satisfaction that it was only three o'clock in the morning.

She was unlikely to sleep again if she started to scroll, which she knew she would, sat there on the toilet. It was something she struggled to resist, however inessential her night-googles might turn out to be.

First Diana checked her emails, then she searched the internet for 4-inch lamé mules, which somehow suddenly seemed imperative.
Soon she succumbed to the ruinous pull of social media and checked each of her various accounts. This held her attention, with barely a blink, for a further 90 minutes.

Next, she had a mild night panic about sleep deprivation and conducted a search for statistical evidence that she might be the sort of person who could exist on four hours (or less) a night. It didn't look promising. She persisted until she found something more optimistic which wasn't connected to prescription drugs.

When Diana's eyes had started to sting, and the sun was threatening to rise, she plugged her phone back into its charging cable and tumbled back into bed, her mind alive and flittering between the injustice of Violet Crock, workplace frenemy, obtaining an additional 20,000 Squareheart followers, and her own inability to track down some purple lamé mules in her size. Diana leapt out of bed and posthumously politically (and reluctantly) 'hearted' Crock's careful photograph arrangement of multiple branded fashion items and the corresponding hashtag catalog that implied she'd been given it all for free.   She then registered for a spin cycling class that would begin three hours later.

Diana dropped her head back on the pillow and felt the pressure of consciously yielding to sleep. She felt fried and defeated and a little bit lonely, but above all aware that the last thing she'd want to do upon waking was to join a spin cycling class full of energetic people.

In what seemed like only moments her phone was emitting the sound of a deep-sea submarine, its way to say it was time to get up. She had a splitting headache, her eyeballs burned, her face felt like the husk of an old summer espadrille, and she definitely did not want to spin cycle. She felt like she'd been through a spin cycle. So much for all of the sprouted grains, steaming greens, liters of filtered water and collagen sachets with which she sprinkled her days.

Wasn't she supposed to feel better than this?

Diana dragged herself back to the bathroom and sat on the toilet, resumed her scrolling, and berated herself for failing to send at least one office related email in the night. Midnight Mailing was popular in her office; a badge of corporate devotion in which Diana frequently felt obliged to partake. The caliber and urgency of Midnight Mailing was usually negligible, and the irony that the most prolific midnight-mailers head-nodded against sleep most days at their desks (and regularly committed vast errors) was lost on everyone.

Plugging in her curling iron, Diana noticed, aghast, that Violet Crock now had another 30,000 Squareheart followers.

Seething, she angrily reached for her toothbrush. It was at this point that she realized she had fallen asleep in her tooth-whitening strips the night before. They had shifted, and seemed to have partially dissolved her gums. Why hadn't she noticed that in the night?

She grabbed her phone and frantically searched 'dissolving mouth' on the internet for advice and nearly dropped the phone in the toilet when a flesh eaten jaw appeared at the top of the search results.

By now Diana had just ten minutes before she needed to leave.

CHOOSE
YOUR
OWN
ENDING

PERSPECTIVE ONE

Diana dressed hastily. She grabbed her coat and perused her shoes. Her eyes landed on a pair of 4-inch silver glitter sandals with whisper thin glitter strewn leather wrap-around (and around and around) ankle straps. They were the sort of shoes for people who don't actually need to walk anywhere, the sort of shoes for people with chauffeurs (of which Diana was not). These, she thought excitedly, thinking solely of Violet Crock and Squareheart, were the shoes for today.

Diana lurched to the elevator. In the lobby of her building she paused and photographed her feet against the beautiful black and white tiled floor. She uploaded the photo right away to

Squareheart, and using her favorite filter and frame, several tags suggesting she'd been given the shoes by the designer as a gift, (which of course she hadn't but Violet Crock didn't know that), and adding a cheery caption wishing everyone a 'glittering day!' wobbled towards the door. Head down, preoccupied, she narrowly missed entanglement with a muddle of dogs attached like balloons on a string to a dog walkers belt, making their merry way back into the building after their morning walk, as Diana, now late, made her less than merry way out.

At work, Diana sat hastily in her cubicle, checking to see if anyone had 'hearted' her post, and trying frantically to loosen the indelible straps of her sandals.

Diana's thoughts were suddenly interrupted by the cold-blooded vein gushing stomach lurching sensation of pure fear that was the inability to remember if she'd unplugged her curling iron, or not. It was this general sense of panic that stayed with her throughout the day. That, and the cold discomfort of her glittered sandals, the straps of which were slowly filing welts into her calves and had lessened circulation to her feet.
What with this and the unsurpassable frustration of Violets Crocks new 'popularity', and the incessant urge to check on her own Squareheart support. It was very hard to focus.

OR

PERSPECTIVE TWO

It was the point at which she nearly dissolved her upper mouth on a tooth whitening strip that Diana realized she had spread her attentions too thinly. Aware that she was entering into a virtual abyss and risked reducing herself to a vapid creature aspiring only to one day photograph her thigh-gap on the island of Mustique, she felt a sudden impetus to change.

Her phone now felt like an evil twin screaming 'pick me up!' 'check me!' 'Look at me now!' 'Let me remind you, in case you could forget, or possibly miss, how much more fun everyone else is having!' '...and how much more popular they are than you!' 'and eating photogenic breakfasts too!' ...and which only let her go when it had had enough of her, and not the other way around.

For all of her hydration, dietary restrictions, leafy greens, crystals, yoga, blood tests and sweat of modern disciplined wellness, she now sensed an intriguing parallel gluttony in phone overuse.

'You would never indulge so much if it came with calories.' Arabella had said, to which Diana had agreed, before being reluctantly placed on Arabella's stringent antidote to Modern Gluttony; The Digital Detox.

THE DIGITAL DETOX

The phones are taking over. But no one is calling. No modern consideration of Hour Ownership would be complete without a glance at cell phone overuse.

When superfluous cell phone usage leaves you with 'tech-neck', repetitive scrolling headaches, fear of missing out, demotion emotions, unfair comparisons, anxiety, logging in...and forgetting why you're there, then it may be time to consider a digital detox.

"What would happen..."

said Arabella to Diana,

"If you treated your cell phone usage like cake?"

You don't devour cake all day every day with wild abandon.

You don't get up in the night to eat it.

You don't care what it thinks of you.

You don't eat it to pass the time, standing in line, or (eek!) sitting on the toilet.

You know that too much is gluttonous

...and unhealthy

...AND UNQUESTIONABLY NAUSEATING

...and also depressingly distorting to your emotions, looks and general...

WELLNESS.

When we Own Our Hours we can appreciate their value. What we make of them is up to us.

CHAPTER THREE

SELECT YOUR PERSPECTIVE

When you Suss the Symmetry you choose your perspective, rather than letting your perspective choose you.

What would happen if you selected an alternative perspective? Could that in itself be enough to impact your experience of this day for the better?

A perspective is a choice. Feeling fulfilled, strong, capable and wholeheartedly optimistic in our dealings with life, or by contrast feeling bitter, resentful, and ready to crumble can all be impacted enormously by the knock-on effects of the various perspectives we happen to take.

It can be quite liberating to consider that a perspective has no shape, or form, no presence outside of one's mind.

.

If a perspective
is a curation of
your
imagination,
emotions
and
experience
then it is
yours entirely
for the taking
and the
shaping into
something
wonderful.

So you can
choose your
own ending
to the story...

.

SELECT YOUR PERSPECTIVE

RILE
AND
REPERCUSSION

What has the power to Rile a Repercussion with the potential to build and impact on your day?

Phone going flat? Not getting your way? Someone stealing your toast in the morning, every morning? Strangers petting your dog? Or patting your baby? Fear? Showoffs? Stress? Interviews? Pressure? Over Exertion? Pollution? Politics? Litter bugs? Fear Of Missing Out? Flabby Thighs? Bloated Tummies? Kids that say the same thing again and again and again and again because they know how much it riles you and find it hilarious? Husbands? Wives? The aging process? Snobs? Moody Strangers looking for a row? Rude people in shops? Supermarkets? Boyfriends? No available parking places? People Pressure? Girlfriends? In-Laws? Lethargy? Greed? Not being able to do up your jeans? Saying the wrong thing? People who don't agree with you? Social Media? Exes? Burning dinner? Snarky comments? Co-workers who don't pull their weight? Family members who don't pull their weight? Always being the one to take out the recycling? Pompous people? Friends that put you in a loyalty conundrum? Television news? Too-tight underwear? The weather? Attitude? Too much Caffeine? Polyester? Hangovers? Embarrassing mistakes? Ridiculous rules? Buying clothes you never wear? Waking up and not having anything to wear? Indecision? Adult push-scooter riders mowing down the walkers on the sidewalk? Parking tickets? Waking up to find a huge pulsating pimple on your chin? Squeezing it and making it worse? Running out of toilet paper? The underwire of your favorite bra breaking free and destroying both the bra and then your washing machine? Not being the 'together' sort of person who hand-washes her underwear? Mistaking cold calling robots for humans? Cold calling robots that pretend to be people? Blisters on your heels? Arguments? Supermarkets selling milk that is already off? Predatory salespeople? HVAC units? Hairs in your food? Over perfumed taxis? Sweaty taxis? Winter in April? People standing you up? Or making you wait? Or not responding to your text messages? Exclusion? Inequality? Forced opinions? Environmental issues? Being so stressed out that you try to remember things you'd never normally even want to remember just to prove you can remember it, and then can't? Diets? Wet towels on the bathroom floor? People who chat when you don't want to talk? Staying in bed instead of exercising and hating yourself all day because of it? Eating someone else's dinner as well as your own and then feeling guilty? Nerves about appointments? Low blood sugar? Constant Interruptions? Other people's mood swings?...

What do
you do
about it?

Strop? Moan? Snarl? Sulk? Stare?
Shriek? Slump?
Mope? Glare?
Wither? Weep? Deflate? Retaliate?
Pass the mood along?

Do you let
a Rile
Repercuss
on the
rest of
your day?

What could you do instead?

...and if you did
it how could the
whole day
be different?

.

THE RILE AND REPERCUSSION OF GETTING THINGS DONE

.

Just as daily blips can blister the day ahead, so can the perspective repercussions of putting off the things we need to do.

We might be afraid or unmotivated to do certain things in life, but if we act with avoidance and the perspective we take is one of immensity, terror, and looming dread, we need to ask ourselves if that isn't possibly worse than just sucking it up and getting things done in the first place.

When the stature we attribute to not getting something done eclipses the effort it takes to do it then the Symmetry is off.

.

SELECT YOUR PERSPECTIVE

REPACKAGING PERSPECTIVES

.

There are the straightforward and obvious Riles and Repercussions in life, and then there are the more subliminal and sneaky thoughts - the ideas we repackage and represent

56

to ourselves to help make those thoughts and ideas seem more palatable and acceptable. These are the things we try and pass off as ok when we know they really aren't. Like when it was your mistake but you don't want to admit it, or when it feels wrong and is easier to swallow under a cuter description. Or when it adds up to present you as someone you'd rather not be. The 'kidding yourself' kind of things.

When we repackage our perspectives the Symmetry is off.

SELECT YOUR PERSPECTIVE

THE
TRUTH
WE
TELL
OURSELVES

We can conjure many slants on the truth, our truth, as we see it, or as we want to see it, and that in turn can also impact our experience of life, because deep down we know when we aren't being honest with ourselves.

Owning it is empowering. Awareness and ownership is essential in evolving perspectives to a better place.

Belief is essential. Think if all of the things that the skeptics say only work because of the people who believe - Homeopathy, crystals, meditation ... Love?

We need to find the truth in our perspectives in order to believe in the power they can conjure.

·

SELECT YOUR PERSPECTIVE

ARABELLA GREENSTOCK

CLIENT TRANSCRIPT

·

Arabella (looks at notes): You're particular about your coffee...

Grace (affronted): No more than anyone else in New York.

Arabella: Too much milk will throw you off your morning...

Grace: I just think that if you're going to have a business selling coffee, and you have a board behind the counter with different options and different prices, then you ought to be able to serve them. It's like being given a pepperoni pizza when you've ordered a margarita. If I ask for a cappuccino, I want a cappuccino.   But, that's not my problem in the morning.

Arabella:...and not a latte?

Grace: Exactly. But, that's not the problem.

Arabella: But you never ask them to make it again. You pay, and you walk away, knowing by the weight of the cup that it's too milky. You're brewing discontent Grace! You berate yourself for not saying anything, then you either tip out half of the coffee and regret the waste, or drink the coffee and regret the milk ... and then, if you are already feeling anxious, you sometimes panic that you're enticing a lactose intolerance. You get to work and snap at someone who wouldn't dare rebuke you, but will, you're suspiciously certain, communicate your misdemeanor around the office, and then you're paranoid, ill-focused, and off balance for the rest of the day. You occasionally give up completely, shattered and withered, and crawl under your desk and cry, and then feel guilty at your loss of self-control.

Do you see the Cause and Effect?

Grace: From a coffee?

Arabella: The Rile and Repercussion?

Grace: Yes, yes, I get it.

Arabella: The Emotional Equation?

Grace (irritated, looks at watch): Yes! You are suggesting my bad day begins with the bit I like best.

CASE STORIES

A TALE OF RILE AND REPERCUSSION

CHOOSE YOUR OWN ENDING

It was with military precision each morning that Grace Slate attended Intensia, the cult Chelsea workout session, and then returned to her Upper West Side apartment to shower, rouse, feed, and usher her children Celeste, Jojoba, and Causeway to their respective schools before arriving at work, coffee in hand, at precisely 8.45am.

Grace was frustrated she could never undercut her timing to 8.40. She perpetually tried to.

Before having the children she'd never been vaguely concerned with her office arrival time, in fact at times she'd relished in the taking of bold punctual liberties. Such was her confidence in her abilities and assurance in her stature that she'd sometimes rolled in at 11am or noon, wearing hangover glasses or swinging a new dress in a shopping bag over her shoulder. But, times change, and with each successive child Grace sensed successive eyes flickering between her, the clock, and the male and non-mother co-workers who were inevitably already established in their seats, screen-gazing their computers (feigning work it might be noted, as most of them were really checking on their social media performance or ordering juice cleanses online).

Nobody actually 'worked' before Grace arrived in the office. Indeed, nobody actually knew why they competed so fiercely to arrive so early.

Grace regarded the morning routine as if an invisible, aggressively athletic personal trainer was following her with a stopwatch. Her time would be announced when she sat at her desk. Lately, marked with a slow and despondent shake of the trainer's invisible head: Failure.

Disappointment.

This, along with the fortune telling coffee set the tone for the day ahead.

This morning had probably been her worst time in a month. She'd done the schools ok, no problem there, no PTA interception which was always a time saver and relief, but, at the coffee shop she'd been stuck for a good five minutes behind a double-width all-terrain stroller. The stroller was attempting a six-point turn, and in the process was clogging the entryway and exit and snagging the cuffs of several chair hung arctic parkas in its path.

Increasingly frustrated at the wait, Grace tried to recite her meditation mantra but found to her frustration that she couldn't remember it.

The stroller-owner was reluctantly unwinding a deflated orange Moncler jacket sleeve from around his front wheel. His pajama clad charge watched cartoons on an iPhone from the blanket padded comfort of the stroller, one chubby clammy hand occasionally dipping into an earthenware pot filled with flaccid carrots and sugar snap peas, only to toss them overboard, unto which they too were ground by the stroller wheels into the Moncler jacket and the coffee-shop floor.

Grace checked her watch and sighed. Her eyes glanced briefly downwards at a silver laptop open on the table beside her. The owner hastily snapped it shut. "Copyright!" He barked defensively, void of complete sentence. "I wouldn't worry." Replied Grace, rather bitchily but well deserved, she felt. Now fully in the grips of Another Bad Day.

Eventually untethered, and without a word of apology for the collective mornings brought to a stand-still, or the damage wrought to the coat which was now patchy with wheel oil, street dirt, and the migrating down of its filling, the stroller owner paused for a sip of his beverage, discovered he had not, as requested, been served a non-dairy, sugar-free alternative, and about-turned back again to the counter, oblivious of his daughter who was now chewing the phone in lieu of the vegetables.

It would be 8.48 before Grace arrived at work today.

She'd tipped out the overly-milky cappuccino in a street-side trash can and her coffee now stood milk appropriate yet mediocre of strength, with a drip hypnotically snaking the length of the side of the cup, inevitably bound for her blouse.

She sat at her desk and...

CHOOSE
YOUR
OWN
ENDING

PERSPECTIVE ONE

She pulled in her stomach, dejectedly peeled back the lid of another packet of seaweed wafers (Grace was a woman who reluctantly subsisted on freeze-dried seaweed snacks) and began a day that would roll on as it began, gradually gaining pace, until she eventually collapsed in an overwhelmed and miserable power suit clad heap at 9pm, only to be woken seemingly moments later, still on the couch, by her 5am alarm call for Intensia, the cult workout, and another day that would roll out exactly as the previous one had before.

OR

PERSPECTIVE TWO

Grace refused for her day to be blighted by a shoddy coffee, inconsiderate coffee shoppers, and smug office early risers. She proudly acknowledged the successful orchestration of her complicated morning schedule and saved some of the good feeling for later, should she need it.

She asked herself what it was about Intensia that kept her going back? Because it was a right pain to get up and get to. She decided that it was; 1) the smug sense of discipline. 2) the exclusivity. 3) the buzz. 4) the music. 5) the camaraderie. 6) that it was hers and only hers in the midst of spreading her time so thin for the benefit of so many other people. Having something entirely for herself felt good and 5am was the only time slot available. Grace decided to make a point of acknowledging the power that Intensia was capable of wielding over her day. The energy it conjured inside her was surely enough to suppress a bad barista, she mused, reconsidering her approach.

From across the office she noticed a co-worker was surreptitiously pumping breast milk at her desk under the tented veil of a Burberry raincoat. The woman was intermittently being sneered at by the smug childfree office early risers, and equally by those mothers who left everything to the nannies, and who as a group combined, were all now doing laps of the room, tapping on phones, and shuffling papers to emphasize their corporate enthusiasm. The woman, suppressing tears of exhaustion and over-extension, had one hand on the pump and the other on a computer. Grace caught her eye and smiled in solidarity, making a note to get the woman a coffee. But probably from somewhere else.

THE
GALACTIC
FORCE FIELD
OF
RESOURCEFULNESS

The Galactic Force Field of Resourcefulness is the collection of tips, tricks, and tools that we can use to empower us and protect us from momentary perspective glitches and the ruts that can ruin a day.

Sometimes this is as simple as the awareness of noticing a bad emotion as it happens and intercepting it accordingly with something better.

Sometimes it can be as a simple as knowing other people feel it too.

Sometimes it takes a more playful approach to divert the mind from darker pre-occupation.

Change should be enchanting. So much of the time positive change is accompanied by a weary sense of deprivation. Perhaps that is a sign that we need to push through to a new perspective. Or perhaps that is a sign that it just doesn't resonate with us and we need something else.

The ideas expressed within the notion of a Galactic Force Field of Resourcefulness follow the principle that if our imagination can take us into unkind places it can equally take us to enlightened

ones.
Silly or otherwise.

The more fun and imaginative the better, to slide the mind into a different place.

So, with that as an introduction, meet the Rut Sucker...

GALACTIC FORCE FIELD

THE
RUT
SUCKER

The Rut Sucker is a self-imagined self-designed imaginary (but nonetheless effective) airborne vacuum cleaner to be used as necessary to suck unwanted thoughts, emotional invasions and negatively impressionable atmospheres away from polluting your perspective.

To make a Rut Sucker, simply imagine a small vacuum cleaner (those little ones that come with the screw-on-the-wall holders are a good starting point shape wise).

Next, imagine its aesthetics. Perhaps it has the face of an 80's heart-throb and roars like a soft top sports car when used.
(- white noise is very effective for a Rut Sucker).
Perhaps it is covered in cherry blossom, or healing crystals, or monogrammed with your initials.
Maybe it comes on automatically whenever you are stuck in a long line with only one person at the checkout.

Maybe it matches your outfit.
Maybe it wears D-Frame shades and buzz brands.

Maybe it is leopard print like mine. Perhaps it's sporty.
Maybe it is bio-luminescent. Maybe it is entirely glitter and utterly blinding in the sunshine.

Maybe it's entirely ecologically responsible. Maybe it's made out of recycled thoughts.

Choose the look and the sound it will make when the symbolic suck is set into action. That symbolic suck being the marvelous occurrence when whatever cloud of unnecessary angst up there in your head is vacuumed out of existence. Just imagine yourself doing it.

BECAUSE
IT
NEVER
EXISTS
IN
THE
SAME
WAY
OUTSIDE
OF
YOUR
HEAD

An imaginary rut sucker, you snigger. Are you bananas, you ask?

Well, sometimes you need to hurl an obscure bit of imagination in the midst to divert the mind from trivial frustrations and nudge the mood to somewhere brighter.

GALACTIC FORCE FIELD

ADVANCING
THE
POWER
OF
RETROSPECT

Another tool in the Galactic Force Field of Resourcefulness is that of Advancing the Power of Retrospect amid minor catastrophe or arduous occurrence. Because, the strange thing is, when we eventually come to recall these events, after the frustration has faded, a miraculous transformation seems to have taken place, for the emotions we felt at the time have evolved into something far more empowering.

'Ah, the power of retrospect!' we say, as we laugh at the time we fell face first into a farmyard pile of manure, lost our luggage at the airport, vomited all night after that romantic oyster dinner, conducted a daunting conversation with a lettuce leaf on our tooth, did an important meeting with yesterday's underwear trailing out of a trouser-leg....

Oh, the memories!

It is quite astounding how something can, in the present, seem quite dreadful, and yet be transformed into an article of humor, entertainment and conviviality once the scorch has paled and the story is ripe to be told and repeated.

Why on earth do we not endeavor to enable some of that positive energy for the present? Now is, after all, when we need it most.

Why wait for it to be in the past when you could have some of the good stuff today?

This is the part where consideration of the 'world out there' is a must. Perspective Power provides further impetus in Advancing the Power of Retrospect. While the notion of Advancing the Power of Retrospect relates to those small to moderate irritations that can throw a day, and while it is not designed to be regarded as a reduction method to temper the significance of the major and painful events we or others might endure, the presence of such a notion is another reminder that experience is an option. We may not have a choice in what we deal with, but we can have a choice when we choose how we experience it as it happens.

CASE STORIES

A TALE OF PINEAPPLE, PEOPLE AND PERSPECTIVES

CHOOSE YOUR OWN ENDING

"First my heel snapped, then it started to rain, then the pineapple broke through the bottom of the shopping bag and the rest of the food fell through after it. I was scrambling around the sidewalk trying to pick it up — nobody stopped to help me — I finally get it all back together - by now I'm holding the broken shopping bag like a hammock and I've got a pineapple wedged into one coat pocket and a jar of peanut butter in the other. And I start to hobble across the street. And out of nowhere an ambulance comes careering around the corner, right through the red light, (no siren), driven by a woman balancing her lunch in a bowl on the steering wheel with one hand holding a fork on its way to her mouth, and of course I scream, and the woman next to me pushing a stroller doesn't notice I'm saving her life and yells at me instead for waking her kid."

CHOOSE
YOUR
OWN
ENDING

PERSPECTIVE ONE

"I yell back at her and everybody turns and gives me the most horrible looks, the bag breaks again and I cry, alone, on Fifth Avenue for ten minutes watching taxi's run over my groceries and being looked down on by pinched faced women in fur coats and leering men in tailored suits."

OR

PERSPECTIVE TWO

"I summon the Advanced Power of Retrospect and I shrug and surpass, feeling mightily relieved that I have not been mounted by an ambulance, and, appreciated or not, have done my good deed on behalf of the defenseless stroller riders of New York. I reward myself with good cheer, even when the pineapple rips through the pocket of my new spring coat and my shopping gets squashed in the traffic."

GALACTIC FORCE FIELD

ADVANCING
THE
POWER
OF
SELF-FORGIVENESS

In the same way that Advancing the Power of Retrospect allows for a swift jump over some of the millstones of the moment, Advancing the Power of Power Self-Forgiveness endeavors to skip the pain of situations you know will eventually fade into a cringe, but which seem so all-encompassing and horrendous as they happen.

Situations which are made worse by the fact that most of us know how to hurt ourselves the hardest.

Sentences we dish out for the likes of being to blame in a petty row.

Or....

GETTING SOMETHING WRONG

Making a silly mistake

EMBARRASSING YOURSELF

Saying the wrong thing

Someone telling you afterwards that you said the wrong thing

SLIPPING OVER OR SLIPPING UP

LETTING NERVES GET THE BETTER

FORGETTING SOMETHING IMPORTANT

MISJUDGING THE BALANCE

Messing Up a Meeting

Using your Rut Sucker to suck up your family

REMARKS THAT DON'T GO DOWN AS THE WITTY REPARTEE YOU HOPED

SMALL BUT BAD DECISIONS

Saying something mean and wishing you hadn't.

Etc etc etc etc etc... It goes on and on and on.

It's life

It happens and it keeps happening all over the world

What doesn't have to happen is to drag the weight of regret around like a months worth of luggage.   Half of the time the realization is bad enough.   Crimes deserve to be punished. Honest mistakes are misdirected energy when they linger in

penance.
Suss the Symmetry of Rile and Repercussion; Own mistakes.
Be empowered. Move on.

WARNING!

Perspectives can change suddenly for the better,
but can also creep back into old ruts when left unattended.
Good perspectives are like plants.
Tend to them carefully
and always leave room in the sunshine for more.

CHAPTER FOUR

TAMING YOUR CONFIDENCE

Confidence. When you have it, you feel electric, then boom! It's one of the first bulbs to blow on the circuit.

A lot of poor perspectives are conjured from frail or faltering confidence that has crumbled as a result of other people's attitudes, off-hand comments, and from bad experiences that have hung around like unwelcome guests, until you're so used to them being there that they start getting their mail re-directed and turning up at the breakfast table and before you know it they've been living with you for fifteen years.

'I'm not confident.'

'my hair is like packaging string'

'I'M UNLUCKY IN LOVE'

'I have the allure of a cabbage leaf...'

73

'I'M NOT CLEVER ENOUGH TO...

'I don't have what it takes to...'

'I'M REALLY BAD AT...

'I have legs like overfilled sausages and look dreadful in this skirt.'

'THERE'S NO POINT IN MAKING MY BED BECAUSE, I AM A HOG.'

'They are all better than me at...

'I wouldn't be any good at...

'I'd love to but...

It is one of life's ironies that those who could do with a dose of harsh reality confidence-deflation rarely partake in the sport, while those who are unfairly self-critical play at the game repeatedly, letting murky labels adhere and become the perfect excuse not to break free from comfort zones, or to question the ruts in which they have us held.

When we are over tired and overwhelmed and hamster wheeling our way through life, there is a chance that our confidence levels, once so self-assured and effervescent, can, when left untended for long enough, either wither into a floaty wisp, forever threatening to blow away for good, or become unruly and unmanageable and quite out of control.

TEMPESTUOUS

Thus, they fail to speak up in our defense, fail to support us in our dreams and ambitions, and wreak havoc with even the most mundane aspects of life out there and getting things done... and then they change their mind and berate us for staying indoors.

Lost Confidence is a pesky electric fence that circles our perimeters and buzzes to remind us of all the things we aren't brave enough to do. But, once in a while, the power goes down, the gates fling open and you're out. Out into the realms of ambition and dream, strength, and determination, potential, and, sometimes...given the wrong source of fuel for your confidence, a misdirected arena of fashion disasters, bad judgement, dancing on tables, flashing your underwear, telling people what you really think of them... (hello Mojito). That, for the confidence impaired, can be enough to further hamper on the inner source of true confidence – the one that doesn't need cocktails or coffee to get going. The one that just believes in you. Because you are you. And that's good enough. The one that accepts you for who you are. That is the confidence to nurture.

It is also important to consider that general consensus pushes us all towards outgoing confidence. Yet, confidence comes with being content with who we are, even if that means admitting and accepting that you have no desire at all to be a social butterfly or the life of the party or to trek across the Himalayas or go to other people's houses for dinner. Only you know if you are holding yourself back, or if you don't want it in the first place. If in doubt engage your Vulturous Assistant.

.

TAMING YOUR CONFIDENCE

DEMOTION
EMOTIONS

.

Demotion Emotions are unfair feelings that erupt and interfere with the day. They can pop up at any time, often when we are tired, and they will try their hardest to occupy our thoughts and downgrade our confidence.

Part of the defense against Demotion Emotions is working out when they are likely to strike - when we are nervous? Tired? Overwrought? Under pressure? Afraid? Feeling Judged?

If your day has turned and you're under self-attack, then ask yourself why you feel the way that you do. Look for reasons other than your self to destroy. Don't accept Demotion Emotions without question or contest.

TAMING YOUR CONFIDENCE

THE SELF-APPRAISAL THEORY

If you were planning to sell your home, would you, or would you not, invite an appraiser to assess its worth and value, having left a thick layer of dust on every shelf, an un-emptied cat litter box, dirty windows, the gentle aroma of boiled broccoli and egg sandwiches in the air... In short, would you present your home for evaluation with a general air of exhaustion? Would it be fair to your home? To your potential sale? Do you think you'd get your true value? The money you need to move on to something better?

If not, then consider this:

Why do we persist in personal self-appraisals when we are tired, stressed, worn-out and with the emotional equivalent of a pedal-

bin full of fish bones and gas-forming vegetables in the house?
Recognize your peak times for self-critical Self Appraisal.

Engage your Vulturous Assistant to take note and consider making it your business to never invite appraisal at these times, and to rely instead on the valuation you conducted at a time when you felt sorted, sussed, and self-assured.

.

TAMING YOUR CONFIDENCE

A HEALTHY DISREGARD FOR BEING JUDGED

.

Taming your confidence also means conjuring a healthy disregard for being judged, or the creepy feeling that we might be being judged by others.

When we care less about being judged we become more self-assured, more self-confident, and more liberated to Suss the Symmetry in life our way.

It could be said that we live in an age of super judgement, and thanks to politics and social media and fervent trends of online posting and commenting we have become an opinion-nation, with more people feeling the right and responsibility to pass public comment and judge the world around them than at any point before in history.

The result of this (one of them) would appear that many people now feel judged themselves.

Accepting the pressure of judgment is a burden that you can choose to decline. You decline it and boom! - the power it held crackling over your head, stopping you following your dreams or doing Life Your Way just withers into insignificance with the zoom and plop of a balloon that escaped before the knot.

When we accept other peoples' judgment as their personal perspectives, and not an overall rule on what goes, and often as a result of their own insecurity, we can let the threat that such perspectives might have had to potentially hurt us, float right out of our orbit instead.

And what about when we are wielding the judgment?

The easiest way to develop a healthy disregard for being judged is to stop judging other people. If 'what you do comes back to you' then it's always going to bite your bra at some time or other.

It's only fair.

CASE STORIES

THE CONFIDENCE CRUSH

CHOOSE YOUR OWN ENDING

Ashley arrived at the restaurant. She had checked her reflection in every window along the way and was still none the wiser as to whether she looked alright. Sometimes, she felt, one could look so often one saw nothing in the mirror at all.

Ashley always got anxious when she went on a date. Dating in New York was merciless. James, whom she'd been seeing for a month, had been openly seeing several other women at the same time as Ashley and had mentioned in passing that three of them were models. The word model left Ashley particularly uncomfortably conscious. She now spent much too much of her time imagining glossy limbs that didn't wobble and pore-less skin.

She was fed up of holding her stomach in.

She was hoping her face was still in place after the wind tunnel walk on Broadway. She was, truth be told, keen to get the date over with and get back to her warm apartment to watch TV. Still, you know, you have to 'get out there' - right?

Despite his overconfidence and rampant womanizing James had a face like a weasel, was brash and obnoxious, and seemed permanently welded to his cell-phone, which he callously referred to as 'the operation center'. To the unfamiliar James was quite ghastly.

It was a cruel chemical reaction of faltered female confidence and the misread assumption that there must be something more to him, (if so many women wanted to date him) that allowed James to interlock with endless dazzling women, each of whom seemed more aware of the threat of being imminently surpassed than of any genuine emotional connection towards James as a person.
Both sides always looked over the other's shoulder for either a threat or something better.

How funny life is.

James ignored Ashley when he sat down at the table. He motioned for 'a minute' with his index finger and, still speaking into his cell phone, beckoned the waiter. "Martini. No Vermouth. Three olives," spliced with "I'm still at work." "I'll be over later." "Wear something good" and an ugly sort of scoff.

Ashley surreptitiously tilted the knife on the table setting to gauge the scope of her eyeliner.

Modern Love.

James reached down and groped her leg. Ashley sighed. She was supposed to be a liberated female, although she failed to see how liberating exactly it was to be acquiescent to a man who was propositioning another woman by phone while squeezing her thigh under the table. 'I suppose I am supposed not to care' she thought. 'If this is liberal dating', she thought, 'I'd rather liberate myself.'

CHOOSE
YOUR
OWN
ENDING

PERSPECTIVE ONE

Ashley resisted the urge to tip James's Martini in his lap, feeling it a bit of a cliché, and a bit of a waste, then realizing James himself was a bit of a cliché, she reached for the glass and drank it herself.

It was such a shame that James didn't notice her doing it. He grappled around for the glass, screen-locked in response to a photograph of a large pair of breasts that had just arrived via text.

Ashley decided it wasn't worth the effort of conjuring another riposte. Instead she taxied home.

Her makeup in her bathroom mirror was intact, but beyond the eyeliner there was a different kind of sparkle. She took a dog-eared novel off her shelf, a romance from the days when one woman was enough. She began to read and ignored her phone, which buzzed across the table with unending messages from James, who now appeared to be quite transfixed by her disappearance.

It would be weeks before she shook him off completely.

The irony.

OR

PERSPECTIVE TWO

Ashley had ample time to consider her response while James composed a lengthy reply to the woman who had sent him her breasts and fumbled around for the ruder emojis.

What did she, Ashley, want, she wondered.
Did she want to empower herself?
Empower 'women'?
Reclaim her confidence?
Reap revenge?
Hurt James?
Embarrass him?
James was a right weasel. Ashley decided that she clearly had appalling taste in men, but she still found him oddly appealing, and practical with it. All of his woman juggling meant that he didn't encroach on much of her time, which she liked far better than some of the overbearing boyfriends of the past. She liked him enough to worry if the other girls were prettier, but not

enough to walk out when he engaged with a topless tart while she sat there at the table.

Oh, it was a conundrum.

It was life.

What did she want?

Ashley decided to ponder it for a while. It clearly wasn't a decision she would answer distracted by her eyeliner.

It was then that the overriding answer arrived. She didn't like feeling driven to feel conscious of her looks, and while the feeling would inevitably erupt again, she had, in this single occasion, the power to change it for the better, and perhaps that would influence the next time too.

Ashley made her hands into fists and panda-rubbed her eyeliner into two great black sorceress swirls. She did nothing to quash the urge she had to emit a tiger-like roar as she rose from her chair. Staid heads turned from tables all around. She held her hands up in panther-like claws. It was bizarre. It felt brilliant. James, aghast, jumped in his seat and while turning around to see if anybody had noticed, knocked his phone on the floor, where it was promptly crushed under the stiletto heel of a thigh-high leather boot worn by a woman bearing the befitting weight of two considerably large breasts, both of which aided in the pressure that led to the smash and decline of the 'Operation Center'.

James looked down at the shattered glass and realized, as he had secretly feared for a while, that his streak might be coming to an end.

From then on Ashley always questioned the roots of her emotions, and never worried about her eyeliner again.

TAMING YOUR CONFIDENCE

A
NOTE
ON
FEELING
BRAVE

So many of us neglect to notice our own confidence because we are too busy zoning in on a single area in which we feel that we are lacking and using that instead as a landmark of our strength.

When we do this we risk completely failing to acknowledge or applaud ourselves for confidence we hold in other areas of life, in ways that, in other eyes would more than eclipse the blip that hangs in the forefront of our estimations.

When we engage a Vulturous Assistant stance, and view our lives from another perspective - with an objective permission to poke - the points we tend to highlight to show we 'can't' come face to face with hard fact proof from the past that we can.

Recall the time that you 'did' - you broke the barriers, you made a courageous decision, you were motivated, organized, self-propelled, you achieved, you put yourself somewhere new and daunting and dealt with it, survived, overcame, came out the other side... Smiling.
You are sure to have proof of ability, of confidence, and of bravery.

We all do and we can all do it again.

.

GALACTIC FORCE FIELD

THE MAGIC CAPE OF NONCHALANCE

.

There are things we care about. There are things we aren't fussed about. There are things that don't bother us. And things that bother us tremendously that we wish didn't matter quite so much to us. Rarely, is an outcome improved, or a situation enhanced by fret and worry and great clouds of nervous energy flowing and swirling all around us and building up into a great storm cloud of emotion.

Get the Rut Sucker out.

A situation will not become magically different through hours, days, or weeks ahead of advanced worrying. They are hours that could be spent making you stronger.

So why do we sometimes do it? Repeatedly?

The Magic Cape of Nonchalance is a magical imaginary cape that allows whatever previously held the unfair ability to throw emotions, meet instead with the great glaze of nonchalance.

The cape is made of a state of mind. It looks as you might imagine it to look, from long and sweeping to short and swinging; this part is aesthetic and can meld to suit your mood (and your outfit).

What is supremely important is the attitude you assume when you put it on. Yes - you imagine this as well. This is the perspective you wish to epitomize.

This is the perspective that says... yes, I acknowledge what is happening.

Yes, I acknowledge the importance of the situation.

Yes, I acknowledge the potential outcome of the situation.

and...

I also acknowledge that nothing will change the importance or ameliorate the outcome if I wither in a state of apprehension.

therefore...

I swirl my cape and consider how I want to carry myself in the approach.

What I will focus my energy on instead.

What will build me up.

What my various choices are for my outlook.

...and what is more in tune with how I want to carry myself through this life.

CASE STORIES

THE TALE
OF
THE
FAKE
GURU

CHOOSE YOUR OWN ENDING

NEWS FLASH!
MOTHERHOOD GURU A FAKE!

The wildly successful parenting handbook; 'The Occupational Hazards of Motherhood' was originally published in the summer of 2006. Since that time, it has found a constant presence in bestseller lists the world over. Selling over 300 million copies, translated into 68 languages, and on its 9th print run, its author, the internationally acclaimed Stella St James, finds herself in constant demand as an authority on motherhood, and makes regular appearances on news panels, chat shows, ticketed events, and breakfast television.

The St James's empire has expanded over recent years to include eye whitening drops called 'Sleep in a Bottle', an odor neutralizing spray called 'Shower in a Tin', and the award winning 'Snazzy Momma Barf Patch' collection of designer self-adhesive fabric squares for covering baby vomit stains on 'Momma's-on-the-fly'.

It is now known that Stella St James is a childless former investment banker who wrote 'The Occupational Hazards of Motherhood' on a blackberry in a succession of international airport lounges.

She was caught on camera this week by an undercover British tabloid newspaper stating that the calculated secret of her phenomenal success is because she noticed after friends and colleagues started having children, that, 'new mothers are easier to bully than the girls were at school.'

This comes the week before the highly anticipated sequel to 'The Occupational Hazards of Motherhood' is released. The book, titled; 'Career Value Zero – In Demand to Inferior' is scheduled, says St James, to 'pick up where 'motherhood' leaves off'.

Stella St James lives alone in Manhattan, New York. She wears nothing machine washable.

The shock had already caused Martine to drop her muffin in her lap. She wasn't quite sure what to do next. There was an eerie stillness to the coffee shop that morning as the news slowly spread around the sleeping strollers that Stella St James was a fake.

Martine's first inclination was to mourn, then to scream, then to feel cheated... they were all huge emotions for a woman who was already exhausted, and it was that realization that led her to sit for a moment longer, muffin crumbled in lap, baby napping in stroller beside her, and consider her options...

CHOOSE
YOUR
OWN
ENDING

PERSPECTIVE ONE

She could ignite her rebound responses. This would fail to do much good other than to release the satisfying vent of emotions she felt. It would certainly trouble the baby, who picked up on her energy. It would probably trigger one of her headaches, which might rage for days. It would undoubtedly render her in a bad mood and looking for someone to pass the dark cloud on to, like a baton in a race, and who would most probably be her husband when he eventually got home that night.

The ongoing power of Stella St James...

OR

PERSPECTIVE TWO

She could conjure a healthy disregard for Stella St James and the months of embarrassingly obsessive devotion and money she had spent adhering to and advocating her every word. She could summon the Advanced Power of Retrospect and try and find the humor that would inevitably come at some point in the future, and enable it now for the present.

She could decide that Stella St James wasn't worth the vast emotional expenditure she could possibly, miscalculatedly, invest in grief and anger. She could Shrug and Surpass, and make a mental leap over the incident to get to something more important, like lunch time... or the overflowing laundry... or remembering to buy lavatory paper.

When Martine thought about it, she realized she'd always thought 'Shower in a Can' was dreadful and the Snazzy Momma Barf Patches were uglier than sick and didn't even stick.

Martine looked at the calm face of her sleeping baby and felt an empowering sense of relief at her interception of perspective. She caught the eye of the mother at the next table who was looking at the cover of her own copy of 'The Occupational Hazards of Motherhood' in horror. "Can you believe it?" Said Martine.

"I followed her every word." Said the woman. "I can recite her manifesto on childbirth, and I did her recipe for placenta omelette, and do a breast milk face-mask every Wednesday..."

"I gave birth in stilettos because of her." Said Martine, slowly shaking her head and emitting a sigh, before they both began to laugh.

On the way out of the coffee shop she ceremoniously dumped her dog-eared copy of the book into the recycling bin. It landed on top of several other copies, more than one of which had been severely defaced with crayon and vegetable puree.

One had been bound into a used diaper.

Martine left quite buoyant. Perhaps she could go guru-free for a while.

She still forgot the toilet paper. Her husband said perhaps she should have kept the book for that.

CHAPTER FIVE

THE SUPPORT ORBIT

Your Support Orbit is the people, places, perspectives, and possessions that support you as you do Life Your Way.

Everything within your Support Orbit has the potential to evolve as you yourself evolve, and as the orbit itself (and the people, places, perspectives and possessions that comprise it also evolves). Some of it will stay. Some of it will change.

FLEXIBILITY

Knowing the potential to change and evolve is to acknowledge and appreciate the moment; to acknowledge and appreciate your

Support Orbit as it stands, right now, and the power it represents to you in your life at this moment.

A Support Orbit uplifts your confidence, enhances your perspective, helps you own your hours, and live life your way.

A Support Orbit is a subjective pursuit. Some people will be inclined to fill theirs with people, others with places, others with possessions, others will mix it up, in varying degrees. The ultimate aim remains the same.

POSSESSIONS?

So many of us are surrounded by landfill levels of tat that it is almost an embarrassment to admit to the power of possessions in an age of over-consumer-indulgence. But, yes, some of it means something. Some of it means an awful lot. So yes, possessions are most definitely included in the Support Orbit. Many of them provide security, support, knowledge, comfort, and transport our perspectives from average to excellent.
Lucky Underwear exists for a reason.

EVOLUTION?

A Support Orbit will evolve according to what stage you are at in your life. If your twenty-year-old summer holiday support orbit was short skirts, friends, loud music, someone with a car, peach schnapps, hunks in nightclubs, sunglasses, no homework, and dancing all night on top of speakers, your post-natal support orbit is more likely other people with similar stitches, a doctor or midwife, pediatrician, coffee machine, washing machine, someone to hug, diapers, and delivery services.

THE SMALL STUFF?

Never underestimate the power of the smaller details in life. If the elevator conversation with the stranger you greet each morning makes you feel like all is ok in the day, then they are, oddly enough, part of your support orbit, although it's probably better not to tell them, or they might never talk to you again.

That said, there is absolutely nothing to stop you acknowledging with appreciation the support you receive from people who won't be scared off to know it. By acknowledging we both convey our appreciation and raise our self-awareness of the potency of their presence in our lives; within in our Support Orbit.

Support Orbits are there to be acknowledged, revered, cherished and reciprocated. As soon as you start to notice their presence you up the power they present.

CASE STORIES

THE TALE
OF
THE
SUPPORT
ORBIT

It was a balmy summer evening in a leafy London suburb, and

nothing could be heard above the cries that rattled the apple trees of one particular garden.

None of the neighbors called for the police, none of the neighbors raised the alarm. They simply closed their windows and opened their laptop computers and resumed their petitions to the council, for the residents of Armstrong-Jones Avenue came home each and every evening to the amplified recitation of pregnant women practicing natural delivery.

Inside the crowded living room of the house in question, a house named 'Ovary,' and under the watchful gaze of several framed photographs of her own 1970's natural childbirth, stood a sprightly woman with a stopwatch who went by the name of Nora Partridge. Nora ran the most popular birthing classes in the whole of London. Her waiting list had run to the hundreds ever since somebody mentioned her in an article in Vogue.

Weaving her way around seven heavily pregnant women, who clung to birthing balls aided by husbands in varying degrees, Nora summoned another contraction.

She crept like a Dickensian narrator, intermittently tending her pot plants, and otherwise warning of the perils of the many dangerous pharmaceuticals on offer at hospital. Birth was an occurrence that varied in Nora's descriptions; from something of an ultimate bliss, to an ordeal of epic and horrific proportions awash with rusty clamps and pulleys, numbing injections shooting in the wrong direction, 'bleeding out' in corridors, reversed gravity, and undue forceps.

Nora moved unaware of the emotional turmoil in her wake. She pulled a rainbow crochet perineum out of her basket of props, and expanding the aged woven mass with her fingers, encouraged her participants to have a 'stretch', explaining in detail the benefits and partnered experience obtained through perineal massage using 'any household' olive oil. Nobody had the stomach to ask what a perineum might be.

Childbirth classes are the ultimate Support Orbit for expectant mothers. You swap phone numbers with other women who very soon will all have found a new and unrecognized time zone and be text messaging at 3am, wondering when exactly it is that hair begins to wash itself, marveling that the pain didn't end in the hospital, and why the modern world expects them to pick up the laundry basket / laptop / car keys and carry right on where they left off when their waters broke the day before, and who can be found subsisting entirely on caffeine, food that requires no assembly or cutlery and can be eaten with one hand, and the support provided by a Bugaboo handle bar.

It can be an immense relief to realize that you are not the only person who can't latch a plastic doll onto a woolen knitted nipple, or who is childish enough to snigger at the pubic forests within the 1970's birthing videos.
It serves as good foundation for when you are ostracized for bottle feeding, or for having your breasts out in public, or undertake an extremely 'natural' pregnancy and twenty-hour natural labor and then get suddenly wheeled into another part of the hospital for an emergency cesarean section. It serves you well when you're the only person who sings 'this little piggy ate roast beef' amid a room full of baby yoga mothers who already know to replace the roast beef with 'nut roast'.
When you 'stay at home' (ie. make your family your work) when everyone else 'goes back to work' or vice versa.

You are in something together. You've got history. You can talk about that, and whatever other embarrassing changes come next. You can laugh. You can summon the magnitude of the power of retrospect to markedly uplift whatever (besides exhaustion) has made you cry; from an inability to take a temperature, to a scolding from a stranger, from mean nurses, to husbands and partners that carry on like nothing has changed (and never get up in the night), to the belief that your identity might, perhaps... have dropped out with the placenta.

This is the power of a Support Orbit. It is a power that can be applied to many situations. It is a power that can be found in many surprising places, for many surprising situations, and one that once it is acknowledged, increases in its ability to support and assist you as you do your life your way, with aplomb, confidence, motivation, joy, and the superlative power of retrospect now.

CASE STORIES

THE
FAUX
ORBIT

CHOOSE YOUR OWN ENDING

'I'm not being bitchy, but...' Ursula prefixed every sentence as if she was issuing a disclaimer.

The group leaned in, their manicured fingers wrapped around glasses holding drinks that varied in strength from vodka soda through wine to water for Jasmine, who was on her second round of antibiotics. But Jasmine didn't need alcohol to get into the spirit of things on moms' night out.

Ursula always set the ball rolling.
The ball would roll with the drinks. It was more of a boulder,

really, and it caught a lot of mothers, husbands, teachers, actresses, singers, political figures, stars of reality television, and the occasional child in its path.

'She's clearly having a midlife crisis.'
'Why she doesn't wax her facial hair, I don't know.'
'I heard she got drunk at Timmy's fifth birthday party and stole Catherine's mother's Chanel purse.'
'I heard she was sick in Catherine's mother's Chanel purse.'
'Have you seen the way her bottom eats her shorts in the summer?'
'Yes - I shudder when I end up on the stairs behind her.'
'Did you know they weren't always called Jill and David? They were 'Hessian' and 'Brownstone' until they were five-years-old.'

And so on. It would continue.

By the end of the evening, Suzy would pull out her credit card, add it to the others in the pile and pay her share of the bill, and so much more, for she left feeling defeated, deflated, double crossing and mean. She rarely slept after a night with the other mothers. She would always wake in a panic at how bitchy she'd become.

Suzy was, admittedly, all for being bitchy when it was well deserved, but Petunia - the object of the annihilation - was really quite nice, and probably had no idea about the mustache - New York City bathroom lighting as it was.

Suzy swallowed two painkillers and a cup of coffee and sighed. In ten minutes she'd need to wake the children and get them ready for school.

Her head pounded.

She considered her options...

CHOOSE
YOUR
OWN
ENDING

PERSPETIVE ONE

She could resign herself to having the sort of friends in her orbit that were always a little bit dangerous. Friends she had ended up with solely on account of the age and school of her kids. Friends she could never quite trust. Friends she'd never call in need, less they talk about it after. Friends who she saw out of ritual and obligation, definitely not celebration.

Some people ended up with great friends, and others got Ursula mused Suzy. Feeling that she was, after all, fairly fortunate in other ways... and you can't have everything...

OR

PERSPECTIVE TWO

Suzy resolved to sort the wheat from the chaff where friends were concerned. A friend, unlike a co-worker, was a choice, and she did not choose to spend her hours on a downward spiral of bitchiness and boredom, ending in a great hungover heap of self-depleted guilt and loathing. Yes, finding friends wasn't always easy, but these women missed the definition of friendship and didn't fit Support Orbit criteria in any capacity.

Suzy went on to excuse herself from enough 'moms' nights out' that eventually, to her great relief, the moms' stopped inviting her altogether, and while she knew all too well that they had started to bitch about her instead, she found such knowledge oddly reassuring. It helped to confirm her decision.

CHAPTER SIX

THE
SUSSED
SIX

"If your imagination can take you to dark places and downtrodden perspectives," Arabella would say to her clients, *"then it is equally capable of the reverse. Why on earth not nudge it along to somewhere better and let it take you to somewhere inspiring and wonderful instead?"*

The Sussed Six is a Six Step Perspective Cleanse. An amelioration station to support the finding, defining, and refining of more empowering perspectives in life, and the overriding of the kind of ruts that can interfere with, and even ruin a day.

It rolls the previous chapters into a juicy and logical routine that can be targeted to a temporary or ongoing blight.

It can be applied to different situations and to different areas of life, and if the process resonates, and gets repeated, it can become an empowering and almost ritualistic ridding routine for drab Demotion Emotions, and a trusty Confidence Booster and useful component of a Galactic Force Field of Resourcefulness.

Based on an acronym, it goes like this:

Step One
S
SET THE INTENTION

Step Two
U
UNRAVEL THE RUT

Step Three
S
SUSS THE SIGNIFICANCE

Step Four
S
SELECT A PATH

Step Five
E
ENABLE YOUR GALACTIC FORCE FIELD

Step Six
D
DROP DEMOTION EMOTIONS

STEP ONE

S

SET
THE
INTENTION

Step One is about deciding what you want your Sussed Six to do.

What perspective is outdated in your life?

Is there an event you need to prepare for in a more optimistic capacity?

Are there some rut-addled responses to be refined?

Is there a reoccurring glitch in your daily routine?

A specific objective?

OR A GENERAL AIR TO SUSS?

IS THERE AN OUTLOOK OUT THERE THAT IS OUTDATED?

A deflating ritual to be tweaked for the better?

WHAT COULD BE IMPROVED?

WHAT IS YOUR GOAL?

What is an altogether more uplifting alternative to the current situation?

And what if you come up with a whole list of things to do?

It can be tempting to attempt a complete life overhaul, but changes can be more impactful and more significant (and therefore more long-lasting) when we implement them individually. One single focus is far more powerful in the rut shaking realms than reams of scattered ideas and intentions all fighting for attention at once.

Too much change rut-ridding wise at any one time can be daunting, overstimulating, or conversely quite boring. That can entice a rebellion streak of resistance, and be simply too easy to give up on - like a giant list of New Year's Resolutions that loses its impact by the second week of January. So, resisting the temptation to tackle everything at once, pick your rut and start sussing.

STEP TWO

UNRAVEL
THE
RUT

The next step in the process is to unravel the rut. To understand and unplug its power, and reduce the influence that it has, for probably far too long, held over life.

Why has it stuck for so long?

HOW DID IT MANAGE TO LODGE UNINVITED?

Was it thanks to someone else?

SOME FRENETIC HAMSTER WHEELING?

Boredom?

IRRITATION?

Influence?

An Outdated Reaction?

LACK OF ENTHUSIASM?

OBSESSIVE TECH RITUALS?

Impaired Confidence?

Fear of Missing Out?

Feeling Judged?

Demotion Emotion?

Maybe it just slipped into the routine unnoticed, undercover and somehow infiltrated its way in a routine of repetition until it found itself accepted and unquestioned?

Or is there something else?

And it's not just about how it got there...

Sometimes unraveling a rut can lead to the knowledge that when we are truly honest with ourselves we might just discover that we actually quite like the ruts we find ourselves in.   Those ruts that give us good reason to complain, or feel sorry for ourselves, or have a good excuse to cheer ourselves up... with a nice glass of wine and an evening spent moaning under the burden of our plight. It can all be quite safe, rewarding, and oddly enticing.

Why on earth would anyone leave all of that comfortable indulgence behind?

When one's Vulturous Assistant implies there might be some rut-addled rewards to some rut-addled responses at play, then we may need to stop rewarding our ruts, and reconfigure our compensation systems towards acknowledgment of progress instead.

STEP THREE

S

SUSS
THE
SIGNIFICANCE

What is important about doing this?

WHAT WILL BE DIFFERENT IN LIFE WHEN IT IS SUSSED?

What will be better?

How will this help?

What is the motivation to get this sorted?

WHAT WILL HAPPEN IF THERE IS NO CHANGE?

What would happen by doing the opposite?

SUSSING
THE
SIGNIFICANCE
OF THIS
CHANGE

Significance equals importance and purpose and meaning and

motive, and, not to dwell on unsuccessful New Year Resolutions, but the lack of sussing some significance around them is a huge reason why so many of them fail - there's just no meaning beyond that endless list of self-improvement demands - nothing to make it personal, or important, or imperative to approach.

Sussing the Significance of a change also allows for some consideration as to what will happen if we don't make a change at all.

Do we want this rut or rile to rage forever?

What does it look like if we imagine the future?

We'll only be older, and still allowing our blood to boil over the small stuff? Still living with sketchy self-esteem? Shifty motivation? The perpetual feeling of being over-done, despondent, or drained? Intermittent confidence lapses still keeping us from our dreams?

What does it look like to imagine the same stuff bugging you for years to come?

Does it add the impetus to intercept?

STEP FOUR

S

SELECT
A
PATH

When you know what you want and why you want it. You need to decide on how to get it.

We sometimes embark on change fairly unprepared, considering the magnitude of the potential it can bring.
Then, in other areas of life, we're all about the prep; who would consider travelling without first thinking 'Aghh! I must pack my toothbrush, passport, underwear, silk-mousseline gown, charging cable, jumpsuit, straw hat, uncomfortable inflatable neck pillow...' etc etc etc? Who??!!
Preparation is key to a Sussed Six too.
A jumpsuit is desirable but not mandatory.

Change should also be enchanting. Whatever the perspective enhancing intention of the Sussed Six Step Perspective Cleanse, there should be some magical, magnetic pull towards the goal and the way that you choose to approach it.

If you can't find a magical pull then you may need to keep looking until you find, at the very least, an angle that intrigues you.
Something about the process and the mission itself should make you feel special, sparkling, unique, and raring to tap your resources and potential with excitement to get going on the future.

Embarking on a Sussed Six Perspective Cleanse should feel like having a new and enormous crush on someone. It's all about perspective, after all.

SO, WHAT CAN MAKE THE CHANGE ENCHANTING?

How can those outdated responses be replaced with new intentions?

WHAT WILL BE THE MOTIVATION TO KEEP GOING?

What rut-addled rewards could be repurposed as prizes for progress?

All questions for a Vulturous Assistant.

and...

How to make the most of this whole experience? You know those stories from the diet clinics of the 1960's where they would just sedate you for a week and you'd wake up thinner? Well, this is not that sort of place. You won't go to sleep and miraculously wake up more Self Aware, more Confident, with a better Perspective on Life Your Way, Less Rut-Addled, Less Automated on the old Outdated Responses. You will live and breathe your life and experience every moment of rut reduction in real time. The power of this potential is in your hands.

Some consideration as to what the experience itself stands to deliver by way of Self-Awareness, Confidence, and Self-Empowerment can aid in both the significance of releasing a rut and the chances of keeping it at bay.

STEP FIVE

E

ENABLE
YOUR
GALACTIC
FORCE
FIELD

What do you have in your Galactic Force Field to support you?

WHAT TRICKS AND TIPS EXIST TO COUNTER A THREAT BEFORE IT ARRIVES?

WHAT DOES THE MAGIC CAPE OF NONCHALANCE LOOK LIKE?

Is there an Air to be Sussed?

Is there a Rut Sucker?

IS IT CHARGED?

Who / What / Where is your Support Orbit?

Engaging a Galactic Force Field of Resourcefulness should be playful.
For example; a nameless client of Arabella Greenstock once found herself riled by the sort of women who cast judgmental

glares and do the old 'up and down' appraisals when they passed her by. Her outdated reaction was irritation and self-doubt, skirt tugging, appearance checking, and a good hour or two of doubted confidence, particularly if the incident collided with existing demotion-emotions or ovulation. Her new response employed her rut-sucker - she simply siphoned those women right up.

"Petty?" she asked Arabella self-consciously.

"Silly?? She wondered aloud.

"Playful? She mused, more confident.

"Effective?" Countered Arabella in return.

- "YES!!! ALL FOUR!!!!"

Engage a Galactic Force Field and have fun with it.

STEP SIX

D

DROP
DEMOTION
EMOTIONS

We own the power to our perspectives, and we can change our perspectives right now. Armed with the right resources we can simply choose not to be riled today and to engage an alternative outlook in its place.

Inspired Emotional Override. It is as easy as that. But keeping Demotion Emotions and poor perspectives at bay requires willpower and practice. Repetition breeds habitual behavior, and sporadic implosions of sketchy self-esteem, low confidence, shifty motivation, or old and cumbersome outlooks can change with time and practice and something better with which to replace them.

When we drop outdated Demotion Emotions it can sometimes be a shock to a system to no longer react in a way it has been used to reacting for a long time.

Shaking the ruts, slants and perspectives that hold us back is a really big deal.

So, do it ceremoniously.
Don't let it slip by unnoticed.

The more stature we place on the ditching of Demotion Emotions the more chance we have of keeping them away.

Note how different life is without an outdated response.

NOTE HOW IT FEELS.

NOTE THE NEW POTENTIAL THAT ARISES.

The moment you read this sentence is in the past.
So too can be outdated perspectives.

Shifting ruts, however silly those ruts might sometimes feel, can make a huge impact on overall confidence, happiness, and the ease at which we make our way through the day, and the impact we make on those around us.

So, take your achievement like a Golden Globe.

Own it. Maybe make an acceptance speech in your head and step back and join your Vulturous Assistant in applause.

THE EPILOGUE OF

ARABELLA GREENSTOCK

The whipping gale and deluge of rain that had forced a tearful Jackie and acquiescent Grayson to concede to the first several hundred of their civil wedding photographs being taken inside the Great Entrance of Dovesworth Hall, between a coat of armor and a procession of hovering English Historical Society general admission guests, had now cleared to reveal a definite flash of clear blue sky.

"Everrrry bodyyyy out!" Screamed Big Sue the wedding planner, using the full capacity of her ample lungs.

Upon the first few shards of sunlight Big Sue had immediately started to herd everybody outside to a particularly waterlogged area she deemed a 'masterpiece backdrop' for the photographs. She said she had seen it used several times before in society magazines, and also once or twice on a television mystery.

Big Sue is known for her attention to detail where the wedding photos are concerned, and we all know why. If Big Sue's brides look astonishingly good in the photographs they usually overlook whatever she forgot or got wrong on the day.

Her tactics are tried and tested. Sometimes she puts prettier guests out of view or in a ditch. Other times she might paste in a couple of celebrities - she carries life size foam-board models of anyone a bride or groom aspires to meet in the back of her van. Sometimes, she'll edit out the sort of people you have to invite but don't really want there, all the while herding everybody outside when the sun teasingly appears and the English stately home selected for the wedding can cease its subsidence into its ancient abashed grounds, and serve its true purpose as backdrop for the photos.

I've been to a Big Sue wedding before. A favor for a budget strapped mutual friend. Sue served sliced white bread and butter triangles as canapés - an ingenious and thrifty move I thought, given the carbohydrate deprived crowd present who fell upon them like caviar blinis after a single glass of champagne. There were several aborted attempts to get the pictures at that wedding, but she gave up when the camera blew away. We all looked like drowned rats, it was freezing cold, and naturally we complained among ourselves with rapture, and yet, when the photos circulated afterwards, Big Sue had somehow superimposed sunshine, retouched everyone's hair and make-up, and added a couple of noteworthy guests. So, after that the consensus became 'what a wonderful wedding it was.' And 'Oh, you should have been there,' and suddenly everybody was serving sliced white bread at parties.

Big Sue, as one might assume by her name, is fairly hefty in stature. She has waist length flat-iron singed hair dyed to a bluish shade of black, several layers of false eye lashes, and a perma-tan that glistens over the canyon of her gargantuan cleavage.

Her appeal is one of a heady mix of sleaze and fear and proves highly effective on the aristocratic gentlemen from Grayson's side of the family, now marching obediently outside, eyes transfixed on Big Sue's acreage as they pass.

They arrive on the sodden lawns outside Dovesworth Hall dazed and content, rainwater soaking upwards of the ankles of their aging Saville Row suits, their rounded thoroughbred wives looking horribly dull, I'm sure, by comparison, whinnying bitchily about the brash, working class wedding planner.

The younger women in the group; those of the London fashion contingent, too green to know about the legend of Big Sue, still occupy a zone of superciliousness, and are lagging behind giggling at her expense.   A few are huddled in the great Dovesworth Hall doorway, mummified in whatever parts of their outfits can be wrapped against the chill, some are trying to hide their hairstyles under their armpits in defiance of the wind, and a few look like they've gone off to hide in the toilets, but not many, because, the truth is, however brash Big Sue might appear, everyone wants to be in her wedding pictures.
"Outside now!" She shreiks at a pretty red head who has paused to write her phone number on a Dovesworth Hall pamphlet for a bearded wandering English Historical Society badge holder.

"I didn't realize he was marrying a man!" Shouts one of Grayson's older, deafer aunties, as Big Sue shunts her outside. "How thrilling!" "But what is this modern fascination with dirty beards?" observes her friend, casting her eyes over the younger males in the group; many of whom appeared to have arrived via time travelling device from some street gang or farmyard of yore by way of Paul Smith or Prada for a suit, and the local boutique hotel for breakfast. "It must be such an adrenaline rush for the young ladies to see what lurks underneath it all when he finally does shave." She mused. "Quite exhilarating...." "...Or a dreadful disappointment." Interjects another equally elderly aunt.   "The beard hides a multitude of sins... and collects them too - is that poached egg or boiled?"

Outside Dovesworth Hall the storm was snaking its way down the valley and towards the expensive and fashionable farmers market which was owned by an entrepreneurial formerly burnt-out London advertising executive. The wind plucked a navy-blue canvas canopy from its stand of brandished leafy greens and released it into the sky like a child's lost balloon.
This was a great thrill to the villagers of Gobsmorth, who intently disliked the bi-weekly invasion of women from giant poorly parked cars, seeking dandelion greens and garlic scapes, while their uncontrollable posh voiced children with matted hair tore up the village untended. The man from the village sweet shop was particularly pleased.

The rousing neighborly cheer could be heard all the way at Dovesworth Hall as a second and then a third canvas canopy was lifted into the sky before bouncing down in succession along a strip of black glossy SUV's clogging up the narrow curves of Dovesglove Lane.

The cheers continued to drift up the valley, and Jackie mistook them for ensemble approval of his Gaston Lawless hat. He assumed such art was a rarity in these parts. He dipped his head so that the remaining Historical Society badge holders might see the delicate taxidermy doves nestled into a mixture of whipped egg white, sea foam, and formaldehyde atop a woven white leather and pewter base.
Gaston Lawless, as everyone knows, is the famous enfant terrible of British millinery. The idea of wearing one of his divine wedding fascinators was probably, if Jackie was honest, his first thought upon Grayson's proposal. The words 'Gaston!' had appeared in Jackie's mind's eye, flashing like the lights around a cabaret club

dressing room mirror, shortly followed by the stalled flight of a white taxidermy dove, so, of course, Jackie had said 'yes'.

An elderly (for most of them are) Historical Society badge holder leaned in for a closer look at the hat, assuming it part of the Dovesworth Hall Nature Trail. She recoiled in terror and fell backwards in several dramatic steps that were finally halted by way of her grasp onto the corner of a Tudor tapestry. This then crashed down engulfing several people in its wake. A large cloud of dust enveloped the expanse of the Great Entrance and for a while all that was visible were the two white taxidermy doves and several upended walking sticks.

The Historical Society badge holder would later enquire as to the availability of the doves in the Dovesworth Hall gift shop, but for now, took to sweeping the dust of decades of English aristocracy from her homemade cable-knit cardigan.
"Are you okay, Fanny?" asked her husband in a muffled voice from beneath the heavy textile. "... I ask because this is quite a piece! I've got my mini rambling torch out of my haversack and I'm reading about it in the guidebook. You should really come back in here and take a look at the intricate craftsmanship. Quite a piece! Quite a piece!"

Fanny sighed and let a bearded, tattooed man in a lemon-yellow suit pull her to her feet, and then took herself off to the refreshment kiosk for a cup of tea leaving Bernard and his mini rambling torch entrenched in tapestry behind her.

Marcus, the photographer, approached the lawn in trepidation.
"I'm just saying, Sue, that my tripod might sink in that mud..."
"If your tripod sinks, Marcus, your career will sink. We both know you're more concerned about your shoes." Big Sue glared at him and turned on her black leather stiletto heel boot, which was ringed with mud and uncut grass, to march the final troops

outside.

"Are you sure about this Big Sue?" Grayson asked in his nervous plummy drawl. "Isn't it a bit... well...windy out here?" Grayson was scared of Big Sue, she was Jackie's friend and Jackie had asked her to do the wedding after she made such an impression on him with the launch party for Hola! Tequila (in which he had encouraged Grayson to invest). Grayson wasn't entirely sure that wedding planning was her forte, but he'd never say so to Jackie, who was extremely defensive of his friends and commissions.

Grayson also wasn't entirely sure that it was appropriate for Big Sue to be wearing a large, black, breast filled t-shirt with the words Hola! and Tequila either side of a large tear that ran from her neck to her navel, but again he didn't say so.
"Look me in the eyes Grayson." Commanded Big Sue, and he did as he was told. Both of them were tall, so this was easily done.
"It's Jackie's big day, and we both want to make him happy." One of her rows of false eyelashes became unstuck and appeared to hang from her face like a flailing rock-climber, it swung in the wind. Grayson stared at her transfixed, zoned out, partly due to the shock of the cold, partly due to her mobile lashes.
"Grayson!" She held her tiger striped acrylic nails in Grayson's face snapping her fingers. "Grayson!" He shuddered and came to. "Grayson, the weather is not going to hold. We need to do this now. Five minutes and we'll have them all back inside."
"Okay." He said and followed Big Sue through the gardens amenably, mouthing apologies to his guests along the way.

"Big Sue to Odette, Big Sue to Odette, come in Odette." Big Sue strode ahead of Grayson, spearing vast amounts of turf on her stiletto heels as she went. "Odette? Odette? Where are you Odette?"

Odette had dropped her walkie-talkie earpiece into the toilet when she'd been reapplying concealer to a large hormonal spot in the center of her chin. Despite being Big Sue's number one assistant, Odette was unpaid and finding their arrangement of remuneration in the form of free Hola! Tequila and experience something of a bind. Big Sue never wanted to discuss the matter either. Secretly Odette had always assumed a job in PR would lead to meeting a celebrity and being swept off her feet and away from her parent's house in Croydon. She was to discover, with dismay, upon her third or fourth day with Big Sue that all of the famous people pictured in magazines attending Big Sue Events were just life-size cardboard cut outs. She repeatedly had to reinforce their heads with duck-tape to add insult to injury. Sometimes she'd kiss her favorites better. Always she'd sigh. Repeatedly, Odette pledged to leave Big Sue, but it was very hard to leave Big Sue.

Big Sue's voice persisted to call Odette. It gargled through the water in the toilet bowl as Odette stared in disbelief. The power of this woman was incredible, she thought, and fished it out giving it a little shake. Should she run it under the hot tap? She didn't really fancy putting it back in her ear.

"My hearing-aid!" An elderly woman in plum velvet, who was clearly from Grayson's side of the family, plucked the device from Odette's extended fingers and pressed it into her ear and tapped. She tapped again. "This doesn't appear to be working. All I can hear is that ghastly woman, and I could hear her without the hearing aid."
Odette was not sure what to do. She forgot about her spot. "Bye, then." She said and hurried off to find Big Sue, who sent her straight to the van to drag seven cardboard A-Lister's through the mud to wedge in position among the guests.

Big Sue clapped her hands above her head several times before remembering she had a foghorn attached to the loop of her black denim waistband. She unclipped it and gave it a honk. The noise sent several older guests careering into a herbaceous border.

"Photos people!" Bellowed Big Sue, possibly louder than the horn. "Let's smile our greatest, nail the suckers, and get our freezing arses back indoors, before we all get blown into Mr Lord Pendlebury's cow shed over there."

Creepy Marcus the photographer snapped away gyrating his hips and bending his knees and grunting with the odd groin based thrust in a style that best suited the soft pornographic material he was most practiced in documenting.

"Just take the pictures, Marcus." Said Big Sue, accompanied by a large crack of thunder.

The winds picked up once again and dragged up the valley a hessian bag filled with garlic scapes and a farmers' market umbrella. The umbrella peaked and troughed in the sky drawing great gasps and sighs from the wedding guests. It dipped down behind Lord Pendlebury's cowshed, and everyone sighed with relief, until it reared back into view and made one final great swoop, before plunging down into the assembled party and slicing a cardboard celebrity's head right off his dashing great shoulders and over the fence into Lord Pendlebury's pigsty.

A few of the more elderly guests had not realized this famous guest was not real, so it came as a terrible fright to see his head ripped clean from his body and sent flying across the country estate. One of Grayson's Great Aunts promptly collapsed in a heap at the shock of it all, at the very same time that another gust of wind tore the taxidermy doves clean from Jackie's Gaston Lawless masterpiece and released them too into the sky.

"Bravo!" Cheered the crowd unaware that this had not been the standard wedding dove release. "Bravo!" they cheered.

Not having noticed the aunt, Big Sue took a bow that she hoped would implicate her services in the success of the proceedings. "Big Sue Events." She said with mock modesty. "Big Sue Events."

Jackie stood in silence with both hands reaching up to touch the holes in his hat. The doves were still up there, circling in the force 5. His natural inclination was to cry and howl with the wind at the loss of the focal point of his three-thousand-pound fascinator, and then to retreat to the private rooms of the hall and redo his face, but people kept slapping him on the back, fashion kissing him, and congratulating him on such a culmination to the wedding so far.

Grayson had been busy attempting to revive his Great Aunt who was incoherently muttering through dry blue lips and hazy eyes. "Should we call her physician?" He asked to nobody in particular. Opening his Aunt's bag to see if there was an address book inside, Grayson was a little disheartened to discover she had pocketed several champagne glasses, most of which were broken in the fall.

"Get your Hola! Tequila shots here!" Called Big Sue arriving on the scene, her hair extensions whipped into an unwitting beehive on the top of her head. Four shot dispensing bottles now joining the fog horn in holsters on her belt. "Hola! Tequila. Get your Hola! Tequila... Then get indoors before you freeze."

Grayson would have asked Jackie if it were necessary to have quite so many references to Hola! Tequila at their wedding, but Jackie seemed so happy now that it seemed unfair to hamper his mood. So instead he busied himself by making a round of the guests, all hastily making their way inside, to thank them for both making the journey and surviving the ordeal of the photographs, and to issue a general promise that from herein it would all get much better.

Everyone milled around for a while, waiting for the sensation to return to their fingertips. We all had that marvelous feeling that comes when something grueling reaches an end. The exhilaration of survival. Nobody yet, had anticipated the speeches or food that lay ahead, we were all just in that magical unexpected place of pause, the one that takes everyone who races through life by delirious surprise when they finally acquiesce to it. An odd unification, for beyond Jackie and Grayson, or Jackie, or Grayson, we, in our little subset groups, had little else in common. Somebody said that they saw a fully-grown sheep, carried by the wind, passing by the window, but it was generally assumed that this was more likely the hallucinogenic properties of the Hola! tequila.

*

Why am I telling you all this? Because it was at Jackie and Grayson's wedding that I first became aware of the power of perspective and the magnificence of self-awareness.

What was your perception of Big Sue? Brash, bossy and hideous? Bold, unique and irreverent?

I looked at Big Sue and I saw complete self-awareness. She wasn't to everyone's taste and she didn't care. She did things her way, with aplomb.

If you think otherwise, then it just goes to emphasize how different our perspectives can be.

I'm not saying I left the wedding wanting to be Big Sue (I left the wedding with hypothermia). I left the wedding wanting to be more self-assured. Someone who had the strength to do what she wanted to do in the world, and to look how she wanted to look. A person who wasn't fazed by supercilious scorn. Someone with a healthy disregard for being judged. Someone who saw no reason to feel inferior to anyone, or to crumble under a lack of confidence. Someone who treated everyone the same, regardless of who they might be, or the stature they might think they deserve.

Big Sue's style is not my style, but it certainly spurred me to find my own. Watching Big Sue I could see that I wanted to evolve into someone who stuck secure to who she was, focused, unfazed among people she knew might be making assumptions. Someone who could see those assumptions were probably there to temper a sense of insecurity. Someone who might realize this, but couldn't actually care, either way, or even bother to feel smug, because her own life was too compelling to step back from to consider the negative trivialities of other people's baggage. Diluting their own personalities to fit in with others. Big Sue just didn't care. She knew it was there and she just didn't care. She did Life Her Way.

People sometimes say they had to 'develop a thick skin', but Big Sue hadn't done that, she was just clearly and totally at ease with the skin she was in. She was self-aware, and with self-awareness comes confidence that the only skin you need is the one that you've got.
I left that wedding in an ambulance (many of us did), wrapped in a silver space blanket, and yet oddly filled with inspiration.

I realized that humans are riddled with perspectives. Everybody there had one, me included; underdressed, frost-bitten, and lurching about in my expensive and ruined sandals as I was, willing, for the most part, the whole thing to be over.

Perspectives are something in this turbulent world over which we can have complete uplifting control in our own lives. This is a tremendous gift, which we should not leave unopened. I could have played that party any number of ways, looking back, as I do now, with the power of retrospect firing my vision.

So, Suss Who You Are, and What You Want, and think about how you intend to Carry Yourself through Life.
Make Balance a Subjective Pursuit.
Curate your own Galactic Force Field of Resourcefulness.
Conduct each day with a steady sizzle of joy.
Conjure a Healthy Disregard for being judged, and for the insta-sludge of comparison.

I returned to New York (when the hospital discharged me) and set to work. I defined and refined my own perspective on the 'bigger picture', and then set up a business to do the same for others.

I served Hola Tequila at the launch.

Arabella Greenstock
Vulturous Assistant
New York City

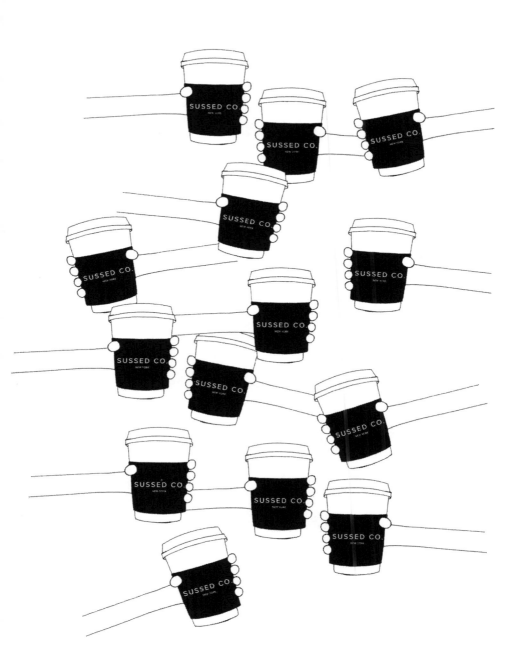

THE SUSSED CO.

GLOSSARY
OF
TERMS

Accept and Respect Flexibility
Positive change should be enchanting and empowering and entrenched in the knowledge that it is in our control. Rule Three in the Vulturous Assistant Employee Handbook

Acknowledge the Small Stuff
When we suss the small stuff the potential for greater change is unleashed. Rule Four in the Vulturous Assistant Employee Handbook

Acknowledgement
To acknowledge is to notice and accept. Acknowledgement in the context of Sussing the Symmetry is to notice, accept, and, where relevant, be grateful.

Advancing the Power of Retrospect

To use the magic that later reflection holds over a frustrating event or occurrence and engage it for use in the present. Why wait until it is in the past? Empower yourself in the present.

Advancing the Power of Self-Forgiveness

To stop punishing ourselves for the little things we fail to do, or over-do, or say wrong, or get wrong. With perspective for the bigger picture we can let go of the small stuff and save our energy for the big things in life.

Arabella Greenstock

Protagonist of the fictitious demonstration of Vulturous Assistant Modern Life Coaching within these pages. She is a figment of perspective designed to illustrate a point.

Auto-Pilot Perspectives

Those perspectives we automatically resort to. Perspectives, which, if they don't serve or empower us, are perspectives to be questioned and possibly evolved into something better.

Awareness

A state of knowledge and perception.

Be Honest with Yourself

Rule One in the Vulturous Assistant Employee Handbook.

Change Should be Enchanting
The Sussed Co. belief that for change to successfully occur it should enchant our senses. It should be personalized and empowering.

City Frazzled
The hectic, draining, consuming state of frenetic city living, and the general assumption that if nobody else ever stops, why should you?
Note: You don't have to live in a city to be frazzled.

Cracking the Code
Understanding the triggers of Rile and Repercussion with regards to perspective and enjoyment of life.

Demotion Emotion
The emotions we have that neither serve nor empower us, but exist solely to bring us down. Often such emotions are conjured as the result of a cauldron full of triggers — lack of sleep, menstrual cycles, over-caffeination, over-indulgence, unfavorable-comparison, unkind commentary, over-loading, frenetic Hamster-Wheeling...

Digital Detox.
A Detox inspired to intercept the fastidious dedication to modern 'wellness' regimes which are so often combined with slovenly and gluttonous approaches to cell phone usage. Presented in the context of comparing phone usage consumption to the incessant consumption of cake.

(to) Drop Demotion Emotions

Step Six in the Sussed Six Step Perspective Cleanse - the bit where you leave outdated automated downward dragging responses and perspectives in the past.

Enable Your Galactic Force Field of Resourcefulness

To make use of the tools we we have at our disposal to shake outdated perspectives and to self empower. Step Five in the Sussed Six Step Perspective Cleanse.
(See Galactic Force Field of Resourcefulness)

Faux Support Orbit

When the people, places, perspectives or possessions we surround ourselves with don't support us after all. Examples of Faux Support Orbits include: frenemies, comfort eating, compensatory habits, over-indulgence and excuses among other things.

Galactic Force Field of Resourcefulness

The amassing of various perspective changing techniques. Use with caution: Imaginations are powerful. Engage your Galactic Force Field only when it is safe to do so (ie. not while driving or crossing the street etc). The Sussed Co. armory includes The Rut Sucker, Magic Cape of Nonchalance, Sussing the Air, and Sussed Six Step Perspective Cleanse, but sometimes all it takes is awareness and acknowledgment of tiny details in life that we might previously have ignored, but which rile a subsequent repercussion of empowerment or joy.
Or, the decision that today you're taking a better perspective.

Hamster Wheeling

The incessant act of going from one task to the next, in sometime fervent self-satisfaction and organization and expectation, all at an increasing rate of physical and emotional self-depletion. Sometimes referred to as 'Frenetic Hamster Wheeling'.

A Healthy Disregard of Being Judged

The art of removing the ego from the realm of judgment. Being judged reflects on the person casting the judgment. Feeling judged is an emotion we can choose to drop.
Shrug and Surpass.

Letter to Yourself

A letter to yourself provides an opportunity to write to yourself from a place in the future – 5, 10, 15 years ahead. Placing ourselves in the future, imagining where we might like to be and how we might like to have gotten there can provide the impetus to get out of ruts and the propulsion to make change.
As featured in the Introduction to Arabella Greenstock, Vulturous Assistant.

Life Your Way

When you stop tuning into everybody else and start listening to yourself.

Magic Cape of Nonchalance.

A key component of the Galactic Force Feld of Resourcefulness, a Magic Cape of Nonchalance is a self-imagined-self-designed (velvet, silk, leopard, sequin, rainbow, lipstick kisses, poetic, mystic...) imaginary cape that you mentally swirl around yourself in support of the ability to shrug and surpass. It has a delicious air of insouciance, is formidable for when you feel like you're crumbling, and a mind game to play to divert oneself from something, somewhere, or someone entirely uninspiring or disempowering.

Modern Day Stresses

Those things that 'get' us, unique to our age or era – mostly digital, mostly socially led or triggered by sensing a lacking by way of comparison. We can lump these stresses on top of traditional stresses (which were usually about far heftier matters than how many 'likes' you got on your new haircut).

Modern Gluttony in an Age of Wellness

For all the juice cleanses, hot yoga, crystals and tongue scraping of the Age of Wellness there is a gaping great parallel gluttony in cell-phone overuse. We often neglect, in our will-powered way, to acknowledge the untended gluttony of checking and scrolling that is eating into our days (and drying our eyeballs).

Multi-Faceted Living

There are so many sides to every story, and there is a modern propensity to add as many as possible, like toppings on a sundae, at any one perceivable time. The irony of 'Having it All' is to crumble under the weight of it all.

Non-Serving

Not a grumpy waiter. Non-serving is a Life Coaching term for behavioral patterns that do not serve us. Things that don't do us good or support us.

Over or Under-Done Hours?

Hours spent on accepted necessities, but sometimes in unnecessary long or short amounts.

Obsessive Tech Rituals

Ever tap in your passcode out of habit and forget why you're there?

One Woman's Mantra

The acceptance that one way does not suit everyone. Balance is a subjective pursuit.

Own Your Hours

Taking ownership of your time. Including the time that you spend dwelling on non-serving or disempowering perspectives. Thinking counts too.

Parallel Hours

Hours spent worrying, growling, scrolling, dwelling, bitching, fretting, fearing, skirting, avoiding - the time we neglect to acknowledge that counts. It still ticks away.

Permission to Poke

The Art of the Vulturous Assistant. Looking at life with fresh eyes, in a fresh way, in a capacity that overlooks excuses and avoidance.

Perspective
An attitude, viewpoint or way of looking at things. Perspectives have the potential to evolve and change our experience for the better. A change of perspective is a magical gateway to a more confident, empowered, potential filled realm.

Ratio of Requirements
We are all unique and we all have a different ratio of requirements in life. The trick is to Suss the Symmetry of what is right for you.

Repackaging Perspectives
The sneaky ability to take something you'd rather not acknowledge for what it really is (usually because it will make you look or feel bad) and gloss it up for greater palatability. Excuses, blame, renaming etc.

Repurposing Riles
The Rile is the starting point. It is the action that sends a ripple of Repercussion throughout the day ahead. To repurpose a rile is to take something that has previously triggered a response of irritation or frustration or wilting confidence (or more) and, with greater awareness and acknowledgement of the power it wields, engage a more empowering response in its place.

Retreat to Conquer
Answering yourself on an empty mind, away from influence. Rule Two in the Vulturous Assistant Employee Handbook.

Riles and Repercussions

A rile is an event or occurrence with the potential to induce a repercussion that can influence further events or occurrences in the day.

Rut

A place to get stuck. A rut in the Sussed Co. context is often a mindset on repeat. Some auto-pilot attitude that holds you back.

Rut Sucker

Part of the Galactic Force Field of Resourcefulness. Another mind-diversion of a creative concept to suck the bad stuff right out of the negative atmosphere.

Select a Path

Deciding how change shall occur. Step Four in the Sussed Six Step Perspective Cleanse.

Selecting Your Perspectives

Sometimes we forget that while we may not always have a choice in what happens to us, we do have a choice in how we experience it.

Self Appraisal Theory

The idea that, at certain times, we might assess ourselves unfavorably. These Self Appraisals then lodge in the mind resisting override from more positive evaluations.
The Self Appraisal Theory proposes that we pledge only to self-appraise when we are feeling fine.

Self-Awareness

Conscious knowledge of ourselves as individuals. Self-awareness can be sorely skipped and shunted aside sometimes in favor of simply getting things done, check! Or by the abundance of opportunities we now have to compare ourselves to other people.

Set the Intention

Deciding what you want to do. Step One in the Sussed Six Step Perspective Cleanse.

Shifty Motivation

When motivation is questioned, you need to question your motivation. How much do you really want to do this? What is the real purpose? What is holding you back? A lack of motivation often signals a lack of resonance on the goal front. Maybe that change just isn't enchanting enough?

Shrug and Surpass

The ability to shrug the shoulders and move on. Especially with regards to situations that previously shook your confidence, left you feeling judged, or incited unfavorable comparison or demotion emotions. These often relate to ego. Shrug and surpass and move on.

Side Affected

To be Side Affected from your Own Success — a result of lifestyle overload. Having It ALL goes beyond the smiling kids, dashing partner, dream job, and superlative footwear... it often includes poor sleep, stress, anxiety, headaches, irritable bowels, questionable confidence, screen induced eye-strain, frenetic hamster wheeling, indecision, exhaustion, always feeling like there is someone to please... and on... and on
ALL means ALL.

Sketchy Self-Esteem

When you just don't feel as good as you deserve to feel. Low self-esteem is often the blight of the undeserved and a prime target for a Rile and Repercussion Vulturous Assistant overhaul. There is almost always a trigger to sketchy self-esteem. Sometimes it's as simple as getting more sleep.

Socially Hectic

The chaotic combination of being ongoingly effervescent and 'out there' both physically and digitally. Self-Awareness is essential to Suss your personal Ratio of Requirements.

Squareheart

The fictitious social media network overused by many of the case story characters in this book.

Subjective Pursuit

A pursuit in life based entirely on personal taste, experience, needs, feelings, and potential.

Support Orbit

The People, Places, Possessions, and Perspectives that support you, inspire you, and help you to do your Life Your Way.

Suss Your Self

To Suss Your Self is to increase your self-awareness to understand Who you Are, What You Want, What You Need, and to decide how you intend to Carry Yourself Through Life.

Sussed Co.

Sam Smith's Creative Coaching Company in New York City.

Sussed Daily Self Software Journal

The next book in the series (also see Sussed System Software). A journal for daily Self Software to set intention for the day ahead.

Sussed Six Step Perspective Cleanse
Six Step 'Cleanse' designed to drop outdated perspective baggage and Identify, Define and Refine a new, more empowering approach to the ruts that can ruin a day.

Sussed System Software
Self Awareness Software found in the The Sussed Self Software Daily Journal. Spits out a daily report comprising answers to the following: This is who I am · This is what I need · This is what is important to me · This is what today needs to be about · This is what I'll do if it doesn't go to plan · This how I plan to carry myself through it all ·

Sussing the Air
The process by which we pick an air, attitude, or someone we admire, list what we admire about them (or it), and wonder whether to carry ourself with one or more of these qualities might be an air with which to empower the day.

Sussing the Symmetry
Cracking the code on what is needed to do Life Your Way.

Suss the Significance
What is important about this? What in life will be better when you have it sussed? Step Three in the Sussed Six Step Perspective Cleanse.

Triggers
The bit that sets it all off.

Uneasy Hours
The time we spent dreading vs doing.

Unravel the Rut
Where did it come from? Step Two in the Sussed Six Step Perspective Cleanse.

Vulturous Assistant
A Vulturous Assistant is that side of your personality with permission to poke and probe an answer from yourself to evoke greater self-awareness, rut removal, and confidence. She is bold. She 'gets' it. She will tell you where to go (because you already know, deep down).

Vulturous Assistant Employee Handbook
Guidelines for Vulturous Assistant protocol.

Vulturous Assistant Report
Putting ourselves in a position to poke, open our eyes, and awaken the urge to shake off outdated behavior and rut-ish thought patterns in favor of something more empowering.

Watching the Cool Girls Crumble

The impetus for this whole endeavor. Fed up of Watching the Cool Girls Crumble; as life overloaded and self-awareness slipped, Sussed Co. evolved and the backlash began.

Note: There are many, many ways of being cool. Far more than are generally given credit.

ACKNOWLEDGMENTS

I would like to thank the following people for being part of my Support Orbit (in many different ways) during the process of building Sussed Co. and the creation of this book:
Jeremy, Barney, & Tabby Smith, Richard & Anne Newman, Michelle Arnone, Mary Ann Ball, Rachel Skinner, Ness, Nige, Sophie & Holly Smith, Marika Zaslow, Yvonne & John Smith, Molly & Dan Miller, Daniella Kahane, Lynda Morling, Lynsi Hughes, Alma Sloan, Ana Garcia, Kathy Sanchez, Melissa Bosomworth, Merci Miglino, Lydia Talpash, Lorna Poole, Sunita Chhibar, Sarah Creek, Abby Struthers, Vicky Booker, Ali Zelenko, Hanh Livingston, Debbie Cartwright, Arielle Childs, Melinda & Michael Paraie, Deborah Townsend, Jeanette Chapman, Sushma Sagar, Lisa Gilbert, Lynda Krasenbaum, Ilene Santo, Meaghan Onofrey, Nicole Allen, Terry Steinberg, Pato Amador, Tillie Mair & Helena Barton.

My Special Thanks to:
Jeremy Smith, Anne Newman, Michelle Arnone, Mary Ann Ball, & Rachel Skinner for reading early copies of Suss the Symmetry and providing such valuable feedback. Michelle Arnone for flying to New York to help me juggle the final phase. Jeremy, Barney, Tabby, (and Harry) for helping me juggle all of the other phases. Ma, for always doing life your way and encouraging me to do the same. Pa, for you unwavering support. Mary Ann and Jonathan Ball for your expert legal advice. And my clients, you are amazing, incredible, and unique, and it is always an honor.
Sam x

ABOUT THE AUTHOR

Sam Smith is the founder of Sussed Co. the New York based creative coaching company where she works with clients to transform their perspectives, release the ruts that hold them back, tame their confidence, and conjure their own unique Galactic Force Field of Resourcefulness.

She is a Certified Professional Life Coach accredited by the International Coach Academy and International Coach Federation, and a Certified Holistic Health Counselor accredited by the Institute for Integrative Nutrition and State University of New York.

She lives with her family in New York.

If you would like to learn more about Sussed Co.

Including

by Appointment Private Coaching

Online Coaching

the Sussed Society Newsletter

upcoming books, events, workshops & more

please visit

www.SussedCo.com

Also by Sam Smith

The Vulturous Assistant Self Software Journal

WHO DO YOU WANT TO BE?

HOW ARE YOU GOING TO GET THERE?

CHOOSE YOUR OWN ENDING

VULTUROUS ASSISTANT NOTES

Vulturous Assistant Notes

Vulturous Assistant Notes

Vulturous Assistant Notes

Vulturous Assistant Notes

Vulturous Assistant Notes

Vulturous Assistant Notes

Vulturous Assistant Notes

Vulturous Assistant Notes

Vulturous Assistant Notes

Vulturous Assistant Notes

Vulturous Assistant Notes

Vulturous Assistant Notes

Vulturous Assistant Notes

Vulturous Assistant Notes

Vulturous Assistant Notes

Vulturous Assistant Notes

Vulturous Assistant Notes

Vulturous Assistant Notes

Vulturous Assistant Notes

Vulturous Assistant Notes

Vulturous Assistant Notes

SUSSED
SELF
SOFTWARE

This is who I am...

This is what I need...

This is what is important to me...

This is what today needs to be about...

This is what I will do if it doesn't go to plan...

This how I plan to carry myself through it all...

This is who I am...

This is what I need...

This is what is important to me...

This is what today needs to be about...

This is what I will do if it doesn't go to plan...

This how I plan to carry myself through it all...

This is who I am...

This is what I need...

This is what is important to me...

This is what today needs to be about...

This is what I will do if it doesn't go to plan...

This how I plan to carry myself through it all...

This is who I am...

This is what I need...

This is what is important to me...

This is what today needs to be about...

This is what I will do if it doesn't go to plan...

This how I plan to carry myself through it all...

This is who I am...

This is what I need...

This is what is important to me...

This is what today needs to be about...

This is what I will do if it doesn't go to plan...

This how I plan to carry myself through it all...

This is who I am...

This is what I need...

This is what is important to me...

This is what today needs to be about...

This is what I will do if it doesn't go to plan...

This how I plan to carry myself through it all...

This is who I am...

This is what I need...

This is what is important to me...

This is what today needs to be about...

This is what I will do if it doesn't go to plan...

This how I plan to carry myself through it all...

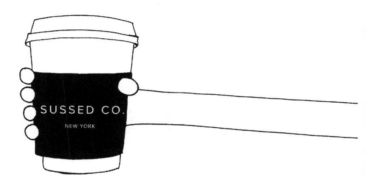

90583285R00113

Made in the USA
Middletown, DE
25 September 2018